Atlantis

Role Playing Simulations
for the Study of American Politics

NELSON-HALL SERIES IN
POLITICAL SCIENCE
Consulting Editor: Samuel C. Patterson
The Ohio State University

Atlantis

Role Playing Simulations
for the Study of American Politics

W. Robert Gump

James R. Woodworth

Nelson-Hall nh Chicago

Library of Congress Cataloging-in-Publication Data

Gump, W. Robert.
  Atlantis: role playing simulations for the study of
American politics.

  1. United States—Politics in government—Simula-
tion methods.   2. Political science—Decision making—
Simulation methods.   3. Role playing.   I. Woodworth, ·
James R.   II. Title.
JK34.G86   1986   320.973'0724   86–5309
ISBN 0–8304–1137–2

Manufactured in the United States of America

10   9   8   7   6   5

The paper used in this book meets the
minimum requirements of American
National Standard for Information
Sciences—Permanence of Paper for
Printed Library Materials, ANSI
Z39.48-1984.

*To our parents,
upon whose shoulders we stood.*

CONTENTS

L I S T   O F   M A J O R   T A B L E S

Atlantis—The New Nation

Simulation 1

Simulation 5

Budget Information for Simulation 6

PREFACE

Every day your fellow citizens in Congress, state legislatures, city councils, school boards, and other public bodies have to deal with problems of maddening difficulty. Decisions have to be made which affect other people, their property, their lives, their well being. In a typical situation, there is no easy answer. There may not even be an answer at all—only a very difficult choice which must be made.

The purpose of the simulations which follow is to expose you to a sampling of these maddening problems, these dilemmas, these difficult choices. It is the hope of the authors that the simulations will reveal to you in a dramatic way through personal experience an understanding of this major point—that whether the subject is writing the basic laws which spell out how authority will be divided or an individual's rights protected, or whether it is dividing up scarce public funds, the dilemmas are difficult and painful.

Perhaps there will not be enough time to use all the simulations. No matter. A sampling of them will reveal dramatically our point.

Acknowledgments

The development of *Atlantis* in its successive versions could not have occurred without the assistance of the support staff of the Office of the Dean of the College of Arts and Science and the staff of the Department of Political Science. Janet Hoelle, Helen Nees, Dotti Pierson, and Jean West responded with unfailing good cheer even when our calls for help were coupled to short deadlines.

The encouragement and support we received from our friends and colleagues made the project possible and enjoyable. In addition, we acknowledge with gratitude the manifold ways in which Dean (later Provost) C. K. Williamson and Juanita King, his administrative assistant, contributed to the success of the project.

INTRODUCTION

Majority Rule—Minority Rights

One of the easiest concepts to state in American government is the principle of majority rule and minority rights, yet it is probably one of the most difficult to practice. We announce again and again that a majority must prevail, yet minorities with deep convictions have difficulty accepting this. For example, public opinion polls have reported that a significant majority of the American public supports gun control legislation. Yet remarkably effective minority action has prevented the majority view from prevailing.

The Equal Rights Amendment provides another interesting example. It failed to pass because it was not approved by three-quarters of the state legislatures. However, it was approved by two-thirds of the members of each house of Congress, by a majority of the state legislatures, and (the polls seemed to indicate) by a majority of American citizens. (While it is clear that ERA failed, and this in spite of what appeared to be majority preference, it is not clear that the failure was attributable to a willful, well-organized minority.)

One might attempt to explain these seeming anomalies as the result of the impact of the federal system, or of representative government, or of well-organized interest groups versus disorganized majorities. Or one might turn to a conspiracy theory, arguing that "powerful interests" somehow are in control. But that is not the point. What is revealed by the cited examples is the difficulty of making majority rule work in practice. The reality seems to be that minorities, not majorities, frequently have their way.

Unfortunately, the other half of the announced principle is equally difficult to carry out in practice. Minority rights is a concept which has been loudly espoused since the Constitution was written. Yet majorities have an unhappy record of trampling on minorities. It is absolutely necessary for my rights to be protected, you understand; it is only your rights which must be subordinated to the public interest. That contradiction is easily justified since my rights are important, moral, and correct; yours are of secondary importance, of questionable morality, and quite obviously incorrect. Indeed, some persons, such as homosexuals and communists, do not deserve to have rights—they are outside the pale. And women do not need to have their rights protected—men can be trusted to do that. Sound familiar? Just within the last three decades, our black citizens have been fighting vigorously to achieve an equality which white citizens take for granted—to vote, to buy or rent a home wherever they chose, to be served in any public restaurant, to gain admission to any university. And a century or so ago it was common for signs on factory entrances in New England to read "No Irish need apply." More than 170 years elapsed between the Constitutional Convention and the election of the first Catholic president.

All too frequently such basic concepts as freedom of speech or freedom of religion are assumed to be freedom for my speech and my religion, not yours. No group seems to be without sin in this matter. Catholics, Protestants, or Jews have all been victims of oppression at one time or another in our nation's history; all seem quite able to forget this fact and use oppressive tactics if the need is great and the cause justifiable. Justice Brandeis pointedly reminded us that "men feared witches and burnt women." Just as is true of majority rule, here too an admirable principle is often difficult to achieve in practice.

In fairness, you should note that often we think and speak in terms of "our rights" when more detached observers would say that the issue doesn't involve any "rights" at all; the issue is simply one of wisdom—what is a desirable public policy? Waving a banner labeled "our rights" and shouting "tyranny" is a tactic that has lost none of its popularity through many decades of use.

The purpose of this book, however, is not to have us condemn ourselves for our failures to live up to our principles but to have you experience the very real tensions which exist in a democracy. These tensions were created by the very principles upon which our nation is founded: majority rule and minority rights, community needs versus individual rights, centralization versus decentralization (or national versus state rights). As you will discover, the words of these principles flow easily for us; the decisions you

will have to make to put life into these principles are often excru-
ciatingly painful.

Why a Simulation?

The previous paragraph stressed that one purpose of this book is
to enable you actually to experience the tensions of democracy. It
is one thing to read or listen to a lecture about the conflict between
majority rule and minority rights, or community needs and individual rights. It is quite another thing to experience it for yourself.
Frequently your role in the educational process is a passive one,
with little learning by doing. The sciences like to insist that students themselves run laboratory experiments rather than merely
watching scientific demonstrations. And that is where the simulation comes in.

What simulations attempt to do, and what we hope *Atlantis*
will do, is to provide the student with an experience which will
demonstrate the principles being discussed. It is one of the social
sciences' answers to the need for a laboratory. A simulation cannot be exactly like the real world, but it is designed to resemble
the real world in certain important respects. It is in fact a simplified version of the real world, including only the essential actors
(roles) and issues to illustrate a point or a principle. Even more
important from a student's point of view, simulations are fun. As
our students never fail to tell us in our course evaluations, the
wonderful thing about simulations is that they keep the instructor
from lecturing!

Keep in mind these points:

- Simulations are (we hope) like reality in selected ways, but
  they are not reality.

- Simulations succeed or fail depending on your willingness to
  be serious about your role and play it realistically.

- This is a learning device, not just a game. Whenever you have a
  chance, ask yourself "What am I learning?" or "What am I see-
  ing?"

- When the simulation is over, your instructor will devote

time to what is called "Debriefing and Critique." Not only is this the most important part of the simulation experience but students consistently report that it is in some ways even more interesting than simulating! During this stage, you will work at answering the question "What did I learn?" After more than 12 years of working with simulations, we can report with some confidence that you will be startled by what you have learned.

Citizen Access to Legislative Forums

Over the years of running simulations on politics we have been struck by the unevenness of student knowledge of political processes. At one extreme of the spectrum there are students who, while in high school, were congressional interns! They can bring a level of understanding and sophistication in the political process which borders on the astounding. At the other end of the spectrum there are students who are not sure whether citizens are ever allowed to speak in city council meetings! In trying to inform the latter group, we may offer comments which are familiar to the more knowledgeable students. What follows is offered in the spirit of helpfulness, but if you find that you need no review, feel free to skip to the next section.

1. Under what circumstances may citizens *be present* at meetings of elected legislative bodies?

   - In the United States, state and national legislatures are very restrictive about the attendance of the public and even exempt themselves from "sunshine laws." Legislatures have firm and rigorously enforced rules about when the public may be present. In fact, the reason representatives of interest groups are called "lobbyists" is that typically such individuals wait in the lobby of the legislature so as to catch senators and representatives on their way to or from sessions of their respective assemblies inasmuch as the legislative chamber floor is restricted to legislators and their staff.

   - Most states have "sunshine laws," which require all meetings of public bodies to be open to the general public any time a majority of the members meets. Executive sessions (closed to the public) may be held if the discussion will involve litigation, personnel matters, or land acquisition.

- At the municipal level any citizen can attend any meeting of the city council, unless council calls for an executive session. However, as in state boards and commissions, executive sessions can be used only in a limited number of situations.

2. Under what circumstances may citizens *speak* at meetings of elected legislative bodies?

- No member of the public is ever permitted to speak to a session of the state or national legislature except on rare occasions when a famous person is to be honored.

- At the municipal level, council sets the rules. Some councils set aside a particular time at each meeting for questions or statements from the citizenry. Other councils permit more latitude and allow public reaction on each issue before council at the time council is considering that issue.

Regardless of the practice followed, the citizen must remember that the meeting is that of the city council in public. It is not a meeting of the public.

Atlantis

Role Playing Simulations
for the Study of American Politics

Atlantis

The New Nation

> One of the problems shared by all new nations is that of creating a feeling of national unity among diverse elements.
>
> Seymour Martin Lipset
> *The First New Nation*

What Is Atlantis?

Atlantis is the name we have given to our mythical nation. As a citizen of Atlantis, you will be involved in a series of short (typically two-day) simulations, rather like laboratory experiments. Your instructor will assign you to a role, in most cases a different role in each simulation. As in real life, some roles will demand more than others, and attempts will be made to let you express preferences for more demanding or less demanding roles.

Now it is time for you, a citizen of Atlantis, to get to work. Each one of the simulations has background information which is essential to understand. In addition, *you will always need to bear in mind that Atlantis is not the United States.* You will want to read carefully what Atlantis and its citizens (you) are like.

Look about you now—at the imaginary Atlantis flag, five interlocking gold circles on a field of green; at your fellow Atlantians; at this strange, but soon to be familiar, place. Are you intrigued? Then read on.

Description of Atlantis

The time is the future. Imagine a nation of which you are a citizen, an influential citizen, a political decision maker. Where is this imaginary land located? It is *not* the United States of America. It is true that many of the circumstances you will experience and the problems you will face will be recognizable, but the purpose of *Atlantis* is to move you beyond the familiar context of community, state, and nation. You will not be able to make your decisions simply as an American participating in the political decisions of the nation, even though the values which guide you will reflect your experience. It would be surprising if this were not so. But you will not have to ask, "What does the U.S. Supreme Court say?" or, "What is the American law on this topic?" The decisions must be made by you and other members of the class and rarely will there be a "right" answer.

What is Atlantis like? When did all this take place? Atlantis was created by the United Nations in the year 1997 by resolution of the General Assembly. Its location, like that of its namesake in Greek mythology, is difficult to pinpoint. Remember, we are dealing with the future, but not the distant future. Thus in principle Atlantis could be enormous space stations, or perhaps it could be inhabitable moons of Jupiter, or huge areas of encapsulated space under the sea. Let us assume, however, that Atlantis is undiscovered land located in the Pacific Ocean, somewhere between Australia and South America. It consists of five very large islands, each one the size of several American states. Each island, as you will see, is a separate culture, with its own value system, socioeconomic qualities, industry, and ambiance.

In the years which followed discovery and settlement of the islands, migration occurred from all over the Earth. Except for the province named Omega, about which you will hear much more later, the provinces are not dominated by any single ethnic group. Very soon after its establishment, a minimal government structure was provided for Atlantis by the United Nations, which did not want the continuing responsibilities and problems inherent in a situation that was beginning to appear all too reminiscent of colonialism. What was not settled, and remains unsettled, is the division of authority and responsibility between the central government and the provinces. Since its formation the central government of Atlantis has possessed few decision-making powers. The provinces, isolated from each other in location, have made decisions on their own without considering the impact on the central government. The province named Omega has always been the most unique in terms of ethnicity and values and thus has been jealous of any attempted incursion into its authority. However, it has now become clear to everyone that a crisis exists. If left to their own devices, the provinces of Atlantis could split apart. The central government does not have the power to prevent secession, in fact it has no power at all.

Below is a brief summary of the principal characteristics of Atlantis.

1. *Life-style:* With the possible exception of Omega, Atlantis citizens in general have a middle-class life-style, with the differences being one of degree. The working class is highly skilled, for the most part, and most of its members have a life-style not

much different from that of the managerial and clerical white collar level. This is in sharp contrast to Omega, where the population is mostly either poor or working class. There is a well-educated stratum in Omega, and it dominates the higher offices of government but is small in both percentage and numbers.

2. *Language:* For all the provinces, English is the official language and, except in Omega, it is also the dominant language. While all the Omegans speak English well, there are several native Omegan dialects.

3. *Religion:* While religious differences exist among the five provinces, these differences, at the time of the Constitutional Convention, have not been a source of major friction or conflict among the provinces. This topic will be discussed later.

4. *Ethnicity:* There is considerable variation both in the number and type of ethnic groups in all the provinces, with the exception, once again, of Omega. In this latter province there is a high concentration of Southeast Asians, more specifically a blending of Polynesians and East Indians.

The Provinces

It is most important to understand at the outset that the provinces are not all at the same stage of development. Even more important, one of them has a totally different history. A brief description of each province is now in order.

Alpha

Alpha, the oldest province in terms of development, is at the stage we now refer to as "post-industrial." Its cities resemble the once bustling metropolises in Ohio and Michigan late in the 20th century. The reasons for the decline are complex, but basically the cause is attributable to changes in technology. In the words of one political scientist, describing similar changes in the USA, the cities of Alpha reveal a hardening of the arteries as each new technology of the means of transportation and production was set in steel and concrete. These ossified remnants of the past for the most part still exist. Alpha's cities, like the 20th-century cities of Ohio and Michigan, have some houses, buildings, and streets designed for a citizenry which walked to work and walked upstairs; other houses, buildings, and streets were built after light rail revolutionized commuting, and technological changes made 10 to 12 stories possible; still other streets reflect the impact of turbo craft, and so on. A visitor from Flint, Michigan, to Alpha City on Alpha would feel very much at home. As has happened in these U.S. cities, Alpha seems to be losing the more educated, the more mobile, the more venturesome; and it is retaining the less mobile, the less educated, the less venturesome.

Given the extensive industrial development on Alpha, it is not surprising that labor unions are an important force, politically and in industrial relations. The major union is of the AFL-CIO type (a federation of industrial and craft unions), and it represents a large part of the labor force.

The citizenry of Alpha is very proud of its heritage, and while some have left to seek their fortune elsewhere, especially in Beta, those who remain are fiercely loyal. There is reason for their pride. [A high level of education prevails, and there are numerous fine universities and colleges.] The people maintain a conservative lifestyle, and religion is a strong force in their daily life. Alpha, as its more conservative residents often say, is a good place to raise a family.

Beta

Alpha's problems are severe enough by themselves, but they are intensified by the existence of the province named Beta. The climate on Beta is much more moderate, industrial development and rapid population growth have come only recently, and the province is blessed with large quantities of capital for investment and the latest in technology. Its cities are new, its citizenry young and industrious, and it is experiencing rapid immigration from the more rural provinces, but especially from Alpha.

In many ways, Beta seems to combine the best and the worst of both Texas and California. New Milano is often compared to Los Angeles, California in the 1950s or Houston, Texas in the 1970s. There has been staggering growth of both industry and population. Not surprising, along with this has come social instability, which manifests itself in a high crime rate and incipient hedonism. The latter is exemplified by the behavior of a "religious" group which calls itself the Nature People, stressing nudity and openly displayed sexual behavior. A storm of criticism from the more conservative elements of Beta has been evoked by the activities of this group. For example, the group has insisted that their children have a religious right not to wear clothes while attending school ("clothing was invented by the devil—God brought Adam and Eve into the world naked and the return to the Garden of Eden will be possible only if people accept nudity"); they argue that school libraries should include books by authors of their persuasion so that children will not be corrupted by all that reading which espouses covering the body with clothing; their places of worship resemble theatres with live sex acts. The Nature People insist that all their activities are protected by the freedom of religion provisions in the Beta Constitution, but (as the "Dilemma of Freedom of Religion" simulation will illustrate) restrictive legislation has been proposed in Beta.

The conservatism of Alpha becomes more apparent when compared with the prevailing value system on Beta. While a conservative element exists and thrives in Beta, the outside world is more attentive to, and seemingly fascinated by, what appears (at least in sensational stories in newspapers and magazines) to be rampant hedonism. News stories about widespread sexual experimentation outrage Betan conservatives and provide self-satisfied Alphans with more evidence of how good life is on Alpha. But conveniently overlooked by its critics is the presence in Beta of a vibrant, churning, dynamic, imaginative population. If one looks beneath the headlines and beyond that which seems scandalous, one discovers a highly educated, talented, sophisticated society. The arts are thriving, and the universities are outstanding. It is true there are some crazies. It is also true that there are winners of Nobel prizes for literature, medicine, and science.

On a different level, and again in contrast to Alpha, unionization in Beta is less important. The unions are smaller and more varied and do not represent as large a percentage of the labor force as in Alpha.

Gamma

The third province, Gamma, is widely known as "the breadbasket of Atlantis." One sees seemingly endless rolling plains of fertile fields profuse with ripening grains. Sparsely populated, these huge grain ranches are enormously productive. Relatively few people are involved in the process, for all the work, from seed planting to harvesting to food processing is handled for the most part by computer-driven machines.

Other areas of the province produce foodstuffs which require more human labor. Depending upon climatic variations, there are fruit-producing, vegetable-producing, and cattle- and sheep-grazing areas. Vineyards produce bountiful harvests of grapes, and the resulting wines are excellent. Land is plentiful, the climate is varied but favorable, and the sparse population is for the most part well educated. These are not the traditional farmers of history; they are overwhelmingly agronomists, computer programmers, meteorologists, accountants, agrieconomists and agriengineers. It is a land of specialists who live in the regional cities located strategically throughout the province. The largest city is Grain City, and it is the home of Gamma Provincial University, known affectionately by its alums as GPU, referred to derisively by its critics as "Hayseed U." If there is a common tone to the people and their values it is one of pride in technical expertise, rather than cultural sophistication. Over a glass of wine the conversation is likely to revolve around crop prices, export markets, design improvements in farm machinery, and computer applications rather than Mozart concertos or Shakespearean sonnets. As a consequence of the enormous export industry, the sparse population, and the highly efficient and computerized agribusiness, the people of Gamma are quite prosperous; poverty is slight. But dissatisfaction exists among the young people, who frequently view life in this cornucopian paradise as a cultural desert. They flee in substantial numbers to the more prestigious universities and alluring temptations of Beta, where the arts prosper and life is more vibrant and frenetic.

Delta

If Alpha can be epitomized by the word "decay" and Beta by "growth," then the word for the fourth province, Delta, is "toil." The people work very hard and often have little to show for it. In some areas rainfall is measured in feet, not inches. As a consequence, a main industry there is lumber. In addition, there is wealth underground in the form of minerals of all kinds, giving rise to the second major industry, mining. Delta's cities reflect these activities. It is a bustling, restless province, with overtones of America's Old West. There is even much talk of rugged individualism. A good way to acquire a black eye and put one's front teeth in jeopardy is to extol the virtues of environmentalism in one of the local bars frequented by miners and lumberjacks. Many of the mines are run by small non-union companies, sometimes family owned, although some large, unionized operations also exist. Thus there is a curious pattern of minimal diversity among the industries of Delta (being primarily lumbering and mining), but considerable variety in the size of the enterprises.

In their values, the people of Delta are among the most traditional of all the provinces. All in all, they have not prospered greatly from that wealth which they export, for the profit too is exported. Many of them spend their lives operating the machines which strip the forests and the mines of riches while gaining only modest incomes for themselves. Fundamentalist, evangelical religions are popular. The favorite beverage is a distilled drink called *eau de mort*, literally "water of death." The Delta version is said to be strong enough to dissolve kidney stones—and kidneys. The drink epitomizes the self-image of the people.

Omega

The fifth province, Omega, is an exception, even an anomaly. A high mountain range runs north and south, dividing the province into two quite different climates. The countryside of the western half of the island has a particularly forbidding and desolate appearance. It is as if one combined the gloomy Scottish moors with the bleak and rock-strewn moonscape of Iceland. The climate is cold and rainy, much like a perpetual month of March in Ohio. The local citizenry have dubbed their land "the snake pit," and it certainly deserves its name. The eastern half of the province is a desert, almost totally uninhabited except for a few nomadic people.

As the decades passed and the population expanded in the western half, the local governments had to provide basic services to the people, including water, sewers, police, fire, and health protection. Communities developed, then cities. Even so, it remains today an uninviting place.

The people of Omega are for the most part poor. Manufacturing is minimal and is composed primarily of cottage industries producing products for local needs. The main industry is subsistence farming. In fact, much of the population spends its time eking out a marginal existence on marginal farms. There are some export industries, one of which is canned fish. The waters in the area are teeming with fish, and a modest fishing fleet and canning industry has evolved. The other export is a particularly strong and bitter, but popular, locally produced beverage called, not surprisingly, Snake Venom. It might be classified as merely a high alcohol malt brew, except that local soils have imparted a strange aftertaste which, we have been told, comes to be an acquired taste. For some reason, perhaps its tendency to provide hallucinogenic reactions, it has some appeal among college fraternities throughout the provinces.

Omega is unlike the other provinces in ethnic characteristics and in its values. The original immigrants were mostly Southeast Asians and Polynesians, and the current citizenry is a blending of these two groups. It takes a determined, rugged person to survive on Omega, thus it is understandable that Omegans are fiercely proud of their self-reliant, rugged individualism. Their history and their life-style make them anti-authority, and they display disdain for formal rules, for social graces. While muggings, robbery, street crime, and rape are rare in Omegan communities, family feuds and killings for revenge are not. In that sense they have a high crime rate. There is an assortment of religions, but Moslems and Buddhists dominate. Religion has not been a divisive factor thus far in the history of Omega.

The picture which thus emerges is of a bleak and unappealing countryside, a mostly poor and not very industrious population except for a small number of educated middle-class officials and professionals, a government marginally effective by design, and a miserable climate. And those are its good points!

Thus, not only is Omega the exception in many senses of the word, it continues to be the thorn in the sides of the other provinces, whose sizeable middle-class populations look upon Omegans with disdain, referring to them as the hillbillies of Atlantis. But increasingly the other provinces need Omega, even if they aren't sure they need Omegans. As the Constitutional Convention issues will reveal, events are catching up with Omega and its highly prized isolation.

The Current Political Scene

It is becoming increasingly clear to the leaders of the provinces that a constitutional crisis exists and that there will be many dire consequences if no action is taken. Delta's provincial legislators, angry over what they feel is the continued exploitation of Delta's resources only for the profit of investors who live on Alpha, Beta, and Gamma, approved a severance tax on all wood and minerals exported from Delta. Gamma responded by placing a similar tax on the export of its foodstuffs. Alpha and Beta are considering retaliatory taxes of some kind.

Another issue is freedom of migration. No one was too concerned about human migratory patterns among the provinces until Omega was added to Atlantis. Suddenly, in response to election slogans of "Keep the Omegees out," the provinces began to establish quotas and income tests, clearly directed at restricting the migration of Omegans into the other provinces.

These problems were bad enough, but then something quite unexpected occurred. An uninhabited, desolate, forbidding cluster of islands, called Erehwon, lies about 90 miles off the coast of Omega. While the islands had been variously claimed by all of the provinces at different times in the past, no province had done more than make noises about "historic claims," "planting the flag,'' and so on. That is, no one had made a move until oil was discovered there. And natural gas. Plus an enormous seam of coal. While each of the provinces could see the promise of these resources, only Omega made a move. And what a bold move it was. The Omegan Navy, consisting of a mixed fleet of tugs and small fishing vessels plus four American war surplus landing craft, landed several hundred men, women, and children. The Governor of Omega announced to a startled world that Erehwon had been occupied by the Omegan militia and a permanent settlement established. Barrels of Snake Venom were visible on the beach of the one natural harbor of the largest of the islands, a certain sign that the Omegans meant to stay.

Even more threatening than the Omegan move, an oil exploration team from a major Third World oil company already has set up shop on another of the islands. It has, in fact, begun to pump and ship oil in significant quantities. What makes this so serious is the growing presence of some foreign troops, ostensibly to protect the oil installations. Yet the daily increase in the weapons and ammunition stockpile, plus increasing numbers of troops, anti-aircraft guns, and helicopters, would seem to belie the assertion that the only purpose is defensive.

The leaders and the populace of the provinces are clearly concerned, even frightened, for the implications of these moves. Five squabbling provinces might themselves become tempting targets for some aggressor in the future, possibly a near future. Although there is little love felt for the Omegans, the leaders of the other provinces cannot bring themselves even to contemplate an armed response to the daring Omegan initiative. And since the Atlantis national government has limited authority, or ability, to respond to the potential foreign threat, all Atlantis can do is protest. They did, however, call for a convention to see whether agreement could be reached to create a national government strong enough to deal with these problems. Even the Omegans understand what all the other provinces have come to realize: they need each other. To break apart and become separate nations is unthinkable. That will only mean a future of trade barriers, suspicion, and growing resentments because of the unequal·distribution of resources and wealth. Even armed conflict is not impossible sometime in the future.

There exists agreement that a constitutional convention must be called and a national government created, but there is no agreement on the details.

Summary

Atlantis is quite diverse. But the variety which exists in topography, rainfall, climate, and natural resources has long since brought about patterns of development revealing areas which can be classified as (1) post-industrial, (2) advanced high technology, (3) agricultural, (4) mining and forestry, and (5) underdeveloped. The politics of Atlantis reflects the conflict of values and conditions among the several areas, and, as will be seen, the conflict shows little sign of lessening. Whether they like it or not, the provinces need each other, and they are being forced by both internal and external events to attempt to create some sort of union with more central authority than now exists.

Table 1: The Provinces of Atlantis

Province	Population (in thous.)	Climate	Soc-Econ Class Structure	Exports	Area (sq. mi.)
Alpha	21,321 (24.9%)	Cold winters (about 5 mos.); hot, humid summers. Rainfall = 35–40″ normal annual.	Full range of soc/econ classes. Much under-employment, esp. in working class.	Machine tools, surface & air transport equipment.	142,748 (14.4%)
Beta	21,149 (24.7%)	Rainy, cool winters (about 2 mos.); hot, dry summers. Rainfall = 10–14″.	Heavy middle & upper middle class.	Advanced tech. equipment—bioengineering.	156,361 (15.7%)
Gamma	17,399 (20.3%)	Cold winters (about 5 mos.); hot, humid summers. Rainfall = 22–25″.	Mostly middle class.	Agric. products; wine, foodstuffs.	234,225 (23.6%)
Delta	15,213 (17.8%)	Mild, snowy winters in mining area; cool, dry summers; mild, wet summers in timbered areas. Rainfall = 11″ in mining areas; 80″ in timber areas.	Mostly working class.	Lumber; minerals.	245,431 (24.7%)
Omega	10,496 (12.3%)	Cold, damp winters of 8–9 mos.; summer is short (2–3 mos.) & is dreary. Rainfall = 30″ annual average, but falls continuously as mist & fog. Western half inhabited.	Mostly poor & working class. Racial-ethnic heritage: S.E. Asian.	Fish & fish products; malt beverages.	214,113 (21.6%)
Total	85,578 (100%)				992,700 (100%)

Creating a
Legislative Assembly

Dilemmas of a Delegate

The fabric of American empire ought to rest on the solid base of the consent of the people. The streams of national power ought to flow immediately from that pure, original fountain of all legitimate authority.

Alexander Hamilton
The Federalist No. 22

Introduction

It generally is agreed that direct democracy is unworkable except in small communities where the entire citizenry can be assembled under one roof for the conduct of the public business and where also the scope of governmental activities is distinctly limited. But when direct democracy is not feasible, then the alternative, representative democracy, presents the would-be architects of a constitution with a host of questions. Should the legislative assembly consist of a single house (unicameral), two houses (bicameral), or more? How many representatives should be chosen? Should they represent geographic areas, clusters of population, economic interests, or something else? And so on.

"That is all well and good," you may say, "for these issues obviously must be settled, but why have a simulation to seek their resolution?" There are at least three points to be made in reply to that question. First, by considering the circumstances and problems of Atlantis, the simulation will help you to see alternatives to the particular choices made for the U.S. political system in Philadelphia in 1787. Second, the simulation will permit you to experience dilemmas and conflicts inherent in an enterprise as fundamental as constitution building. Finally, the simulation will offer opportunities for you to improve your skills in managing conflict.

There is one piece of information that you need to bear in mind as the simulation begins. It is clear that the sentiments of most delegates to the Atlantis Constitution Convention favor the establishment of a chief executive elected by direct vote of the people. A parliamentary form of government, like that of Britain, is not in the cards. The details of the chief executive's powers and responsibilities will be worked out later by the convention, but the realization that the chief executive will be elected by popular vote has clarified the thinking of many delegates with respect to the legislative assembly. Nevertheless, many questions remain to be decided before the Atlantis Constitution will have a workable set of provisions regarding a national legislative assembly.

As you begin the simulation you will observe that a series of issues has been identified for resolution, and a brief discussion of pros and cons appears immediately below the statement of each issue. Other arguments probably will occur to you, but you have already at hand sufficient information to begin.

Constitutional Convention Delegates: Then and Now

The American Constitutional Convention of 1787 provides an interesting model for us. The number of representatives in a state delegation varied enormously, and the number seemed to bear no resemblance to the state's population or to anything else. Some delegates declined the appointment; some accepted but never arrived; some arrived and then left early; some arrived late. The following list reveals the remarkable imbalance:

Table 2: Number of Delegates Appointed by the States Represented in the Federal Convention*

From		Attended	Signed
New Hampshire	(4 appointed)	2	2
Massachusetts	(5 appointed)	4	2
Rhode Island	(no appointment)	0	0
Connecticut	(3 appointed)	3	2
New York	(3 appointed)	3	1
New Jersey	(7 appointed)	5	4
Pennsylvania	(8 appointed)	8	8
Delaware	(5 appointed)	5	5
Maryland	(5 appointed)	5	3
Virginia	(8 appointed)	7	3
North Carolina	(7 appointed)	5	3
South Carolina	(4 appointed)	4	4
Georgia	(6 appointed)	4	2
	(65 appointed)	55	39

*Reprinted from *Journal, Acts and Proceedings of the Convention Which Formed the Constitution of the United States*, John Quincy Adams, ed. (1819), pp. 13–15. As reprinted in *Documents Illustrative of the Formation of the Union of the American States*, (Government Printing Office, Washington, 1927), pp. 85–86.

An even more interesting and significant fact about the American Constitutional Convention is that each delegation only had *one* vote. Often the larger the delegation, the more difficulty there was in finding agreement. The search for consensus, therefore, had to take place at two levels—first within a delegation and then among the delegations. The arguments, the bargaining, the sometimes harsh words, are the stuff of legends.

The Atlantis Constitutional Convention follows the format of the events which took place in Philadelphia in 1787. The issues you will deal with will thrust you into the middle of questions about division of authority and of responsibility. In this simulation, as in 1787, there is considerable variation in the number of delegates per province, and the variation is not related to population. Since each delegation has only one vote, the number of delegates neither increases nor decreases delegation influence.

The size of your class will determine the number of representatives in each delegation. Your instructor will distribute a list of names which identifies the representatives in each of the delegations.

Here are some rules to keep in mind:

1. For the voting on all subsidiary motions preceding the final vote (such as amendments, motion to close debate, etc.) *each representative may vote.*

2. On the final vote on each of the simulation issues, regardless of the number of representatives, each provincial delegation has only *one* vote. Each delegation must determine how that vote will be cast. In other words, any motion which, if adopted, will have the immediate effect of adding language to or deleting language from the draft Constitution must be voted *by delegation*, each delegation having one vote.

3. A delegation vote may be split in half, but not into fractions smaller than half.

4. You may play yourself, but *you must not take positions which would be unrealistic for a representative for your province.* Other than that, you are free to use your own best judgment. When in doubt, ask yourself, ''What is the plausible way to behave?'' Follow a rule of reasonableness.

The Simulation

Perhaps you already have noticed that each of the first two *Atlantis* simulations has as its setting the Atlantis Constitutional Convention. However, though the setting is the same, the issues of each simulation are quite independent of the other. Throughout this first simulation we will fix our attention on the problems and issues encountered by constitution framers when they must address the task of constructing a legislative assembly for a new nation.

Stage One: Selecting a Speaker

Your instructor will begin the simulation by identifying a location in the room for each delegation. The representatives of each delegation will then gather at these locations and seat themselves. It will be helpful if the representatives within each delegation introduce themselves to each other.

The first order of business is for each delegation to choose someone to be spokesperson. No more than five minutes will be used for this.

Next your instructor will announce that the Atlantis Constitutional Convention will meet in plenary session, which means that the entire assembly will meet as a single group. Your instructor will now identify one of the representatives to be Speaker Pro Tem of the convention. That individual will move to the front of the room and preside until the convention elects a permanent speaker.

At this time your instructor will identify the nominees for the permanent position of Speaker, and the Speaker Pro Tem should write their names on a blackboard, if one is available. The Speaker Pro Tem will then state:

> "The Atlantis Constitutional Convention is now called to order. The first order of business will be the selection of a Speaker of the Convention."

The next action is to have an election for Speaker. The following procedure is a simple one to use:

a. The Speaker Pro Tem will call on each candidate to stand up, identify himself or herself and the province represented, and state how he or she will carry out the task of Speaker of the Convention.

b. Blank ballots will then be passed out, one to each representative. The Speaker Pro Tem will instruct the assembly to write a single name on the ballot. (For the purpose of choosing a Speaker, *each representative may cast a ballot.*)

c. The ballots should be collected and two members of the convention identified to tally the votes on the blackboard. The person getting the most votes wins. In case of a tie vote, the winners will toss a coin.

d. The Speaker Pro Tem will announce the results of the voting and request the newly elected Speaker to preside. (Applause for the new Speaker is a nice gesture.)

e. The first order of business for the new Speaker will be to appoint (not elect) a recording secretary. (The secretary will keep simple *minutes,* recording only *actions* of the convention. That is, each motion offered will be recorded, plus everything which happens to that motion—approval, defeat, sent to committee, vote count. *No debate, no discussion will be recorded.*)

Stage Two: Running the Simulation —————

NOTE: A brief explanation of the principles of Parliamentary Procedure is located in the Appendix. You will find especially useful for reference during the simulation run the Rank Order of Commonly Used Motions (p.219) and the Sequence of Motions chart (p.219).

1. The Speaker will state:

"The first order of business of the Constitutional Convention concerns whether the national legislative body shall consist of one chamber, or more than one. The delegations will now be given a maximum of three minutes to caucus before opening the floor to a motion."

Then the Speaker will ask, "Do I hear a motion regarding

the number of legislative houses?'' Following the placing of a motion on the floor, discussion and possibly amending motions will ensue.

When the Speaker believes that the convention is ready to vote, the Speaker will ask, ''Do any of the delegations wish to caucus before the delegations cast their votes on the motion?'' If requested, a three minute caucus will be allowed.

The convention votes on the pending motion (each delegation casting one vote), and the Speaker announces the result.

Things to Keep in Mind: *Number of Chambers*

a. A single legislative chamber can have some advantages:

- Costs should be less since there are fewer legislators and support staff.

- Bills should move more rapidly through the legislative process because there is only a single legislative body to consider the proposed laws.

- Public attention may be able to focus more easily on a single body, and thus citizen interest in civic affairs may increase.

- The relationship with the executive branch should be simplified since there is only one set of legislative leaders.

- Voters may be better able to hold the legislators responsible for their actions because there is not a second legislative body upon which to shift blame. A favorite technique in two-house legislatures is for one of the houses to pass a piece of legislation to appease constituent pressures, confident that the other house will rescue them from error by defeating the bill.

b. Two houses also offer advantages:

- Deliberateness, not speed, is a very important quality to consider in the legislative process. Hastily considered legislation is almost invariably bad legislation. Therefore, two houses are better than one, and important problems or consequences are far more likely to be uncovered when bills are thoroughly reviewed, thoroughly researched, and thoroughly considered.

- It will be more difficult for the executive branch to gain control of both houses. Separation of powers requires a strong and independent legislature. A two-house legislature thus is better able to resist executive domination.

2. When this issue has been resolved, the Speaker will state:

"The next order of business is the question of how the house(s) shall be apportioned. Shall it be on the basis of area, population, or something else? The delegations will now be given a maximum of three minutes to caucus before opening the floor to a motion."

Then the Speaker will ask, "Do I hear a motion regarding how the house(s) shall be apportioned?" Following that the discussion and possibly other motions will ensue.

When the Speaker believes the convention is ready to vote, the Speaker will ask: "Do any of the delegations wish to caucus before the delegations cast their votes on the motions?" If requested, a three minute caucus will be allowed.

The convention votes on the pending motion (each delegation casting one vote), and the Speaker announces the result.

Things to Keep in Mind: *Apportioning the Representatives*

If you create a representational system which allocates legislators in proportion to population, then only numbers of people are being considered. Yet we know that people are more than mere numbers. People divide up by socioeconomic class, by religion, by economic interest, and so on. Area representation or economic interest should be considered. Some activities, farming for example, require large amounts of land and not many people. If only numbers are considered, then the vital role played by farmers and the huge investment they must make may well be ignored or even harmed by a much larger number of voters in that district.

3. When this issue has been resolved, the Speaker will state:

"The next order of business is to determine the number of representatives in the representative body (or bodies). The delegations will now be given a maximum of three minutes to caucus before opening the floor to a motion."

Then the Speaker will ask, "Do I hear a motion regarding how many representatives shall be in the representative body (or bodies)?" Following that the discussion and possibly other motions will ensue.

When the Speaker believes the convention is ready to vote, the Speaker will ask, "Do any of the delegations wish to caucus before the delegations cast their votes on the motion?" (If requested, a three minute caucus will be allowed.)

The convention votes on the pending motion (each delegation casting one vote), and the Speaker announces the result.

Things to Keep in Mind: *Number of Representatives*

a. Another difficult decision revolves around the question of whether there should be only a few representatives or many. It seems clear that a larger number of representatives enables one to provide representation for more and smaller groups of people. But it is a dilemma somewhat similar to that faced by those who devise representational systems for cities. Each minority group wants its interest represented on council. For example, in Cleveland, Ohio, it is not surprising, given the large number of different ethnic groups in that city, that at one time there were 33 members on the Cleveland City Council. But when each group is represented on council, how does one get council to consider city-wide concerns? That was part of Cleveland's problem. The council was often accused of being overly concerned that each ethnic group was represented and protected; no group seemed able to lift its sights to larger issues. Even the mayor's office was viewed as a position to be passed around among the dominant ethnic groups.

b. If one provides for a smaller number of representatives, then one representative has to represent a larger number of people, which almost always means a greater variety. Yet in a democratic and heterogeneous society no one group can dominate; therefore compromise is necessary. The differences, whether they be religious, economic, socio economic, or ideological, have to be accommodated. The question for you, the creator of the new constitution, is where the accommodation should take place? If you have fewer representatives, then more of the bargaining, the compromising, will take place *prior* to election, at the time candidates are nominated and during the campaign; if you have more representatives, it is likely that more of the bargaining and compromising will occur within the legislature.

---

4. When this issue has been resolved, the Speaker will state:

"The next order of business is to determine how long terms shall be and whether they shall be staggered or run concurrently. The delegations will now be given a maximum of three minutes to caucus before opening the floor to a motion."

Then the Speaker will ask, "Do I hear a motion regarding how long the terms shall be and whether they shall be staggered or run concurrently?" (It should be pointed out that these are two separate questions, and it may be the preference of the convention to treat them separately.) Following that the discussion and possibly other motions will ensue.

When the Speaker believes the convention is ready to vote, the Speaker will ask, "Do any of the delegations wish to caucus before the delegations cast their votes on the motion?" If requested, a three minute caucus will be allowed.

The convention votes on the pending motion (each delegation casting one vote), and the Speaker announces the result.

Things to Keep in Mind: *Length of Terms*

a. The question of length of terms is rather closely related to a topic you may encounter later, if your instructor chooses to use Simulation Four: the trustee model versus the instructed delegate model of representation. At issue is whether a representative should respond to the wishes of constituents or whether the representative should rely upon his or her own best judgment, regardless of constituent feelings. Obviously, the shorter the term, the greater the difficulty for a representative to exercise independent judgment, for the purpose of the short term is to require the representative to return to the voter frequently. A short term is, in effect, a voter's short leash on his or her representative.

b. A second aspect of the short term, and related to the example just given, is the cost of frequent elections in terms of both time and money. In the case of a two-year term, a representative has to begin to think about and run for the next election almost as soon as the term begins. This means frequent commuting between the location of the legislature and the home district to maintain constant voter awareness of the representative's activity. Constantly running for reelection also means constantly looking for money to pay for all the campaigning, and the people who can most easily be tapped for funds are the special interests. It seems that, the shorter the term, the greater the vulnerability to special interests—whether these be the dairy industry, labor unions, or opponents of abortion. The converse, of course, may also be true. Longer terms seem to enable representatives to be freer from the influence of special interest pressures simply because elections are less frequent and thus are somewhat less likely to be fought over a single issue.

c. A related decision has to do with whether all terms of office run concurrently or are staggered. If the terms run concurrently, a large shift in voter sentiment can result in a sizable portion of the legislature being defeated in an election and the resulting risk of losing experienced leadership. The good and the bad are immediately apparent. The advantage of a clean sweep is that when the voters have indicated a policy change is needed, the legislature is able to reflect that demand quickly. The old guard is gone. The staggered term concept would have enabled a third, or a half, or some fraction of the body to change, but not everyone. The assumption is that this enables change to be more deliberate, more considered. One hears the argument for conservatism, for making haste slowly. The U.S. Congress combines the two concepts, as you recall, keeping the House of Representatives closer to the voter with short terms which run concurrently, and giving the Senate longer, staggered terms, more removed from immediate voter influence. What do you want in your legislature?

Stage Three: Debriefing and Critique

Your instructor will inform you when this is to begin.

NOTE: Your instructor may ask you to complete and turn in the evaluation form on the following page.

Evaluation Form **Simulation One**

1. In comparison with other courses, or portions of courses, which you have taken, how would you rate this simulation experience?

2. What do you consider to be the most important thing (or things) you learned from the simulation?

3. Was there anything about the simulation which you found disappointing?

4. Do you have any suggestions as to how the simulation might be improved?

5. Suppose a friend had a choice of introductory American Government sections, one of which used simulations such as the one you just experienced. The friend asks you whether he or she should choose the section offering the simulation. What would your advice be?

Please indicate whether your role was:
_____ Very active (Was a spokesperson for provincial delegates, or the speaker, or was an outspoken delegate.)
_____ Moderately active (Spoke once or twice, but was not very involved.)
_____ Slightly active (Active only within the delegation discussion.)
_____ Inactive (Observed the events. Did not really participate in them.)

If more space is needed, the opposite side of this page may be used. If you wish to suggest changes or improvements in the simulation, please do so. Thank you.

National Needs
and Provincial Preferences

Dilemmas of Allocating Powers

*Measures will too often be decided to
their probable effect, not on the
national prosperity and happiness,
but on the prejudices, interests, and
pursuits of the governments and
people of the individual states.*

James Madison
The Federalist No. 46

Introduction

Suppose that you were to attend a political science class tomorrow and the instructor were to begin by saying, "Today we'll discuss centralization versus decentralization." Would you be sitting tensely on the edge of your seat, eagerly awaiting the revelations contained in the instructor's next words, or would your reaction be distinctly more restrained? Now suppose instead that in your next class the instructor were to say, "Today we are going to talk about capital punishment, the availability of abortions on demand, whether mothers should be given custody of the children in most divorce cases, and how to improve the quality of basic education in the public schools." Would your chances of staying alert and attentive be better in this latter class? Now, a final question: Would you believe that after the first fifteen minutes or so the discussion easily could be the same in each of the two classes described? It's true, for the "problems" discussion in the second example will have to consider *where* these various matters are to be decided, that is, at what level of government should a particular type of decision be made. That is simply another way of stating the choice of centralization versus decentralization, national versus provincial rule.

Perhaps you doubt that it matters much one way or the other. If so, consider these questions.

1. If there were a proposal to locate a nuclear power generating plant about five miles southwest (i.e., upwind) of your home, would you prefer to have the final approval or disapproval of the location made by the national government, by your state government, or by local government?

2. Where would you prefer to locate the regulation and enforcement of air pollution laws—at the national level, the state level, or the community level?

3. Would it be preferable to have high school teachers licensed by the national government, by the states, or by the communities?

4. Where should drunk driving laws be made? Where should they be enforced?

5. Should your state have the power to regulate transportation of radioactive wastes on all highways within its borders?

Because these questions do matter and similar considerations mattered at the Constitutional Convention in Philadelphia in 1787, a simulation was developed, having as its object the enhancement of your understanding of the tensions created by the competing claims of centralization and decentralization.

In this simulation the questions cluster around the issue of how responsibility and authority are to be distributed between the national government and the smaller units, called provinces in Canada and Atlantis, and called states in Australia and the United States. Who gets to do what? Does the authority of the central government cover all areas of governmental activity? Or just certain ones? If the central government has been given authority, is its power exclusive? Limited? Shared? This is only a sampling of the questions.

The topics are troublesome enough when you read about someone else having to deal with them. Now the problems will be yours. Depending on the role you have been asked to play, you must decide what will be in the best interests of both your province and the nation. Perhaps you will discover that the interests and needs of both your province and your nation must be kept in some kind of balance.

Locating Decisions—Which Level of Government?

Most of you have encountered somewhere the terms unitary government, federation, and confederacy. These terms are used to describe the location of formal authority within political systems. For example, Britain and France are unitary nation-states: the formal authority to adopt policies, no matter what the topic, resides in the national government. Lower level governments in Britain and France have only such authority as the national government chooses to give them. By contrast, a federation, the earliest example of which was the United States, gives the national government powers on some topics (e.g., national defense, regulation of foreign and interstate commerce, coining money, postal service) and leaves the rest to the states or to the people. (Examples are the regulation of marriage and divorce, regulating the curriculum of public schools, and setting credential standards for teachers.) Sometimes the authority in a federal system is overlapping, as it is with respect to road-building or the apprehension and prosecution of drug importers and distributors. In that case each level may have the authority to proceed, and important problems of adjustment and cooperation appear.

Of course, the Constitution framers of 1787 did not travel to Philadelphia muttering to themselves, "We ought to have a federation." They convened because the national government established under the Articles of Confederation was too weak to sustain itself. They sought a stronger government, but neither public opinion nor the obstacles posed by geography would have permitted a unitary system; that was clear at the outset. So the framers assembled their proposed new Constitution plank by plank in response to specific needs and concerns and compromises, and only later was the label *federation* invented and applied to this new type of government, a government which was something of a hybrid—born of necessity and fathered by political ingenuity.

The term *confederation* refers to an apportionment of powers in which the national government's scope is quite limited, consisting chiefly of matters pertaining to defense and foreign relations. The experiences under the Articles of Confederation prior to 1789, when the new Constitution went into effect, and the experiences of the Confederate States of America during the Civil War suggest quite clearly the limitations of a confederacy in coping with modern conditions. But remember that the differences among these three types—unitary government, federation, and confederation—are differences of degree. The differences lie in the size of the array of topics given to the national governments for policy determination. Decisions concerning the apportionment of powers between or among levels usually reflect the distinctive traits and circumstances of that particular nation. Such decisions are more likely to stem from intensely pragmatic concerns than from ideological predispositions.

The diversities characterizing Atlantis (and described in earlier sections) may suggest to some delegates the wisdom of attempting a federation. However, the *Atlantis* simulation is not based on some preconception of what would be best. On the contrary, regardless of what decisions you finally make concerning the apportionment of powers in Atlantis, you must face the dilemmas inherent in choosing between national needs and provincial preferences.

Stage One: Selecting a Speaker————————

If your class has already engaged in Simulation One, then each delegation has chosen a spokesperson and the convention has selected a Speaker. Your instructor will indicate if these delegation spokespersons and the Speaker are to continue in office or if new individuals are to be chosen. *If new individuals are to be chosen, turn to pages 19–20 for the procedure.*

If your class did not engage in Simulation One, *it is essential that you begin this simulation by reading the Introduction and the background information (pages 1–13) and by following all the steps outlined on pages 16–18.*

Stage Two: Running the Simulation————————

NOTE: A brief explanation of the principles of Parliamentary Procedure is located in the Appendix. You will find especially useful for reference during the simulation run the Rank Order of Commonly Used Motions (p. 219) and the Sequence of Motions chart (p. 219).

Below you will find selected provisions for the proposed new Constitution of Atlantis. The Study Committee on National Powers has just reported these recommended provisions to the Constitutional Convention. There is a feeling within the convention that the Study Committee on National Powers contains within its ranks a large proportion of members favoring a very strong national government, but be that as it may, the Report of the Study Committee is now before the convention. Some corridor criticism has been expressed that insufficient attention has been given to the preservation of provincial authority and responsibility.

Your instructor may indicate that only some of the provisions will be considered, or the instructor may indicate a sequence of consideration different from the sequence in which the provisions are presented.

The following proposals for the Constitution of Atlantis have been offered by the Study Committee on National Powers for approval or rejection. Amendments may be offered at any time prior to a final vote on each item.

The delegates have already agreed to the following provision offered by the Study Committee on National Powers. As will be recognized, it is similar to the "necessary and proper" clause in the American Constitution. The Atlantis section will read:

> The Legislative Assembly of Atlantis shall have the power to make all laws which shall be necessary and proper for carrying into execution the following powers and all other powers vested by this Constitution in the Government of Atlantis or in any Officer thereof.

You probably will find that the language of this "necessary and proper" clause helps you to interpret the proposed sections which follow.

Proposed Section VI. Paragraph 1:

The Legislative Assembly of Atlantis shall have the power to raise and maintain military forces for the common defense and to guarantee to each province a democratic form of government. In implementing this provision the Legislative Assembly of Atlantis shall have the power to conscript males of the age of 18 years or older.

The Speaker will state:

> "The next order of business of the Constitutional Convention concerns the power to raise and maintain military forces. The delegations will now be given a maximum of three minutes to caucus before opening the floor to a motion."

Then the Speaker will ask, "Do I hear a motion regarding the question of whether the national legislative body shall have power to raise and maintain military forces and conscript males of 18 years or older?" Following that, the discussion and possibly other motions will ensue.

When the Speaker believes that the convention is ready to vote, the Speaker will ask, "Do any of the delegations wish to caucus before the delegations cast their votes on the motion?" If requested, a three minute caucus will be allowed.

The convention votes on the pending motion (each delegation casting one vote), and the Speaker announces the result.

Things to Keep in Mind: *Providing for the Common Defense*

a. Some capacity to provide for the common defense seems to be an essential quality of governments everywhere. The absence of this capacity in the United Nations, for example, helps to explain why we employ terms other than "government" when speaking of that organization.

b. This proposed paragraph also addresses the possibility that at some point military authority might be needed to put down domestic insurrection or violence. Is that desirable? Is it better to have armed forces which lawfully can be used only for defense against threats from outside?

c. The significance of the conscription power can be understood more fully by examining the history of the Civil War in the United States. In April of 1861 the U.S. had a very small (15,000 men) standing army; the Confederacy had none. Eventually the increasing scale of the war forced both sides to institute a draft, but the Confederate government's resort to a draft was especially ironic inasmuch as it demonstrated the strong centralizing pressures of a war being fought against centralizing trends in Washington.

d. Question: Is this sentence about conscription needed? If you think that conscription is a power needed by the national government, could you rely on the "necessary and proper" language (see p. 33) as linked to the power to "raise and maintain military forces"? Or must it be stated explicitly?

Proposed Section VI. Paragraph 2:

The Legislative Assembly of Atlantis shall have the power to establish a National Police Force which shall have sole authority to enforce the laws of Atlantis and of its provinces, except that each province may establish and maintain a highway and coast patrol for the purpose of enforcing its vehicular and water craft regulations.

The Speaker will state:

> "The next order of business of the Constitutional Convention concerns the power to establish a National Police Force and a definition of its jurisdiction. The delegations will now be given a maximum of three minutes to caucus before opening the floor to a motion."

Then the Speaker will ask, "Do I hear a motion regarding the question of whether a National Police Force shall be established which shall have the sole authority to enforce the laws of Atlantis and of its provinces, with exceptions as noted?" Following that, the discussion and possibly other motions will ensue.

When the Speaker believes that the convention is ready to vote, the Speaker will ask, "Do any of the delegations wish to caucus before the delegations cast their votes on the motion?" If requested, a three minute caucus will be allowed.

The convention votes on the pending motion (each delegation casting one vote), and the Speaker announces the result.

Things to Keep in Mind: *National Police Force*

a. Law enforcement, except for provincial traffic regulations for land vehicles and water craft, will be in the hands of the national government.

b. Critics may wonder whether the National Police Force can be relied upon to enforce laws of a province's legislature. Does this enforcement arrangement give the government of Atlantis an effective veto (either by intention or by neglect) over the laws of the provinces? What if a province wishes to have more vigorous law enforcement efforts and wishes to have more resources committed to law enforcement? Can this be done?

c. Defenders of the paragraph may point to a greater potential for effectiveness and efficiency if an integrated national police force is established. Variations in enforcement levels, lower professionalism, perhaps even corruption, are risks thought by some to be avoided by the proposal as it now stands.

Proposed Section VI. Paragraph 3:

The Legislative Assembly of Atlantis shall have the power to impose and collect taxes. Except as otherwise provided in this Constitution, no province shall impose or collect any tax on a source taxed by the Legislative Assembly of Atlantis without the express consent of that Assembly.

The Speaker will state:

"The next order of business of the Constitutional Convention concerns the power to impose and collect taxes. The delegations will now be given a maximum of three minutes to caucus before opening the floor to a motion."

Then the Speaker will ask, "Do I hear a motion regarding the question of the Legislative Assembly of Atlantis having the power to impose and collect taxes?" Following that, the discussion and possibly other motions will ensue.

When the Speaker believes that the convention is ready to vote, the Speaker will ask, "Do any of the delegations wish to caucus before the delegations cast their votes on the motion?" If requested, a three minute caucus will be allowed.

The convention votes on the pending motion (each delegation casting one vote), and the Speaker announces the result.

Things to Keep in Mind: *Power to Tax*

a. The first sentence probably will not evoke opposition, for a government that lacks the power to tax is not much of a government at all, as the history of the Continental Congress under the Articles of Confederation demonstrates.

b. But does the second sentence, in its effort to give primacy to the needs of the national government, give too much? Does it perhaps give to the national government the ability to elbow aside the provincial government's tax needs?

c. How persuasive is the reply that reasonable decisions and responses to needs will be made by national and provincial legislators as events unfold? If you are not persuaded, what alternative language should be adopted?

d. A severance tax—i.e., a tax on natural resources extracted from the earth—has been in other nations a significant revenue source for provinces and states rich in mineral and oil resources. Might the Atlantis Legislative Assembly, by enacting a small tax on severance, preempt and foreclose severance taxes imposed by a province? If so, is that objectionable, or is that acceptable?

Proposed Section VII. Supremacy of this Constitution:

All laws made under the authority of this Constitution shall be the supreme law of the land. Any dispute or controversy arising under this section or the section preceding (Section VI) shall be decided by the Court of the Union of Atlantis. (Note: It has been decided already that this shall be an 11-member court whose members are elected by the Legislative Assembly to 11-year, staggered terms.)

The Speaker will state:

"The next order of business of the Constitutional Convention concerns the question of the supremacy of this Constitution.

The delegations will now be given a maximum of three minutes to caucus before opening the floor to a motion.''

Then the Speaker will ask, ''Do I hear a motion regarding the question of the supremacy of this Constitution?'' Following that, the discussion and possibly other motions will ensue.

When the Speaker believes that the convention is ready to vote, the Speaker will ask, ''Do any of the delegations wish to caucus before the delegations cast their votes on the motion?'' If requested, a three minute caucus will be allowed.

The convention votes on the pending motion (each delegation casting one vote), and the Speaker announces the result.

Things to Keep in Mind: *Supremacy Clause*

Without the first sentence of this section the Atlantis Government would be distinctly weaker and therefore more like a confederacy. Any effort to apportion authority between two levels of government requires that the respective allocations of power be written down somewhere (usually in a constitution), and any such writing inevitably will give rise to uncertainties and disputes concerning its proper interpretation. The critical question is who will decide these inevitable disputes? A court? A legislature? And should the decision maker be a component of the national government? Of the provincial government? Is there any way to ensure an objective decision, or must the ''referee'' inevitably be a member of one of the competing ''teams''?

Proposed Section IX. Limitations on the Legislative Assembly:

No appropriation shall be made which will cause expenditures to exceed revenues for that fiscal year unless the Legislative Assembly has, prior to the appropriation and by the approval of not less than $3/5$ of those members duly chosen and sworn, declared a state of emergency and authorized the amount of the deficit.

The Speaker will state:

''The next order of business of the Constitutional Convention concerns limitations on the Legislative Assembly's power to borrow. The delegations will now be given a maximum of three minutes to caucus before opening the floor to a motion."

Then the Speaker will ask, "Do I hear a motion regarding the question of limitations on the Legislative Assembly's power to borrow?" Following that, the discussion and possibly other motions will ensue.

When the Speaker believes that the convention is ready to vote, the Speaker will ask, "Do any of the delegations wish to caucus before the delegations cast their votes on the motion?" If requested, a three minute caucus will be allowed.

The convention votes on the pending motion (each delegation casting one vote), and the Speaker announces the result.

Things to Keep in Mind: *Balanced Budget Requirement*

There are at least two issues in this provision, both of them issues of wisdom or judgment. First is the question of whether a balanced budget should be mandated by the Constitution, and second is whether an exception should be permitted provided that an extraordinary majority ($3/5$ of the total membership) approves.

Proposed Section XII. Powers Reserved to the Provinces.

Paragraph 1: Each province shall have the power to impose and collect taxes on products transported into the province from any other place.

The Speaker will state:

"The next order of business of the Constitutional Convention concerns the power of each province to impose and collect taxes on imports. The delegations will now be given a maximum of three minutes to caucus before opening the floor to a motion."

Then the Speaker will ask, "Do I hear a motion regarding the question of the power of each province to impose and collect taxes on imports?'' Following that, the discussion and possibly other motions will ensue.

When the Speaker believes that the convention is ready to vote, the Speaker will ask, "Do any of the delegations wish to caucus before the delegations cast their votes on the motion?" If requested, a three minute caucus will be allowed.

The convention votes on the pending motion (each delegation casting one vote), and the Speaker announces the result.

Things to Keep in Mind: *Provincial Power to Tax Imports*

This provision guarantees one type of tax resource to the provinces irrespective of the language of Section VI, Paragraph 3. There is a question of wisdom concerning the power of a province to enact a tariff on the products imported from another province. What do you think?

Paragraph 2: Each province shall have the power to establish such rules and procedures regulating the entry of persons into the province as may be deemed appropriate, provided that the entry of visitors for stays of less than 90 days shall be subject to regulation only by the Legislative Assembly of Atlantis.

The Speaker will state:

"The next order of business of the Constitutional Convention concerns the power of each province to regulate immigration into the province. The delegations will now be given a maximum of three minutes to caucus before opening the floor to a motion."

Then the Speaker will ask, "Do I hear a motion regarding the question of the power of each province to regulate immigration into the province?" Following that, the discussion and possibly other motions will ensue.

When the Speaker believes that the convention is ready to vote, the Speaker will ask: "Do any of the delegations wish to caucus before the delegations cast their votes on the motion?" If requested, a three minute caucus will be allowed.

The convention votes on the pending motion (each delegation casting one vote), and the Speaker announces the result.

Things to Keep in Mind: *Provincial Control of Immigration*

While this provision gives authority over foreign tourists to the Atlantis Government, the provinces will be free to choose their settlers. If you are an Omegan, how does that strike you? If you wish to see a strong and united Atlantis, how does that strike you? If you are a Betan, sharing in your province's comfortable climate and robust prosperity, how does that strike you? And so on.

Stage Three: Debriefing and Critique————

Your instructor will inform you when this is to begin.

NOTE: Your instructor may ask you to complete and turn in the evaluation form on the following page.

Evaluation Form **Simulation Two**

1. In comparison with other courses, or portions of courses, which you have taken, how would you rate this simulation experience?

2. What do you consider to be the most important thing (or things) you learned from the simulation?

3. Was there anything about the simulation which you found disappointing?

4. Do you have any suggestions as to how the simulation might be improved?

5. Suppose a friend had a choice of introductory American Government sections, one of which used simulations such as the one you just experienced. The friend asks you whether he or she should choose the section offering the simulation. What would your advice be?

Please indicate whether your role was:

_____ Very active (Was a spokesperson for provincial delegates, or the speaker, or was an outspoken delegate.)

_____ Moderately active (Spoke once or twice, but was not very involved.)

_____ Slightly active (Active only within the delegation discussion.)

_____ Inactive (Observed the events. Did not really participate in them.)

If more space is needed, the opposite side of this page may be used. If you wish to suggest changes or improvements in the simulation, please do so. Thank you.

Needs and Rights in Collision

Interests and Actors in the Policy Process

The right of property should be sacredly guarded, but we must not forget that the community also have rights, and that the happiness and well being of every citizen depends upon their faithful preservation.

Chief Justice Taney
*Charles River Bridge v.
Warren Bridge* (1837)

Introduction

A friend of ours tells the anecdote of being in London and witnessing a pedestrian tossing a candy wrapper on the ground. Another person picked up the wrapper and shouted at the culprit, "Stop that! That's just not British!" Revealed in this anecdote is the rather remarkable difference in the cultural values of the United States and England. But even more, this homely illustration calls attention to the conflict between individual rights and community preferences. This simulation attempts to have you, the student, struggle with this conflict between individual rights and community needs or preferences at a far more profound level than the discarded candy wrapper. The simulation will introduce you to several interrelated topics: the policy process, the newer uses of eminent domain (some of which may startle you), and a case study based on events in Detroit, Michigan in the 1980s. With this as background, you will then find yourself participating in a very difficult decision-making process.

The Stages of the Policy Process

The term *policy process* in the title of this simulation is less mysterious than it sounds. It is a shorthand way of describing actions (i.e., policies) the government decides to take and how it came to be that one particular action was selected rather than another. Although it is not difficult to understand the concept, the process itself is complex. In the paragraphs which follow we have developed a summary of the policy process by drawing heavily on the thoughtful work of James E. Anderson in *Public Policy Making*[1], where policy is defined as "a purposive course of action followed by an actor or set of actors in dealing with a problem or matter of concern."

The process starts with someone's idea. The someone could be the president or a member of the Cabinet, a governor of a state, a mayor, a member of Congress, an angry tax payer, a mother whose child was killed by a drunken driver, or almost anyone who wants action of some kind. Or it could be one of the several thousands of interest groups which want everything from a tariff to protect the market for products to a subsidy to protect the price of a particular crop. Or it could be a group opposing the federal funding of abortion; the list of ideas for governmental action is limited only by the desires of human beings. In every case, the citizen or spokesperson for an interest group (or governmental agency or political party) is saying "there ought to be a law." This is the policy initiation stage. The goal is to get the appropriate agency of government to consider that proposed law, that policy.

Out of the multitude of ideas calling for governmental action, only a small number ever get serious consideration by either the general public or a governmental body. Anderson refers to this as getting on the "policy agenda," meaning "those demands that policy-makers either do choose or feel compelled to act upon . . ."[2] Why do some proposed ideas for action (i.e., proposed policies) get considered while most do not? There seems to be no precise answer, but it may be helpful to think of the question in terms of a checklist of possible reasons.

1. Was the policy proposed by or supported by someone in a leadership position? The point is that presidents, governors of a state, or mayors of a city often have direct access to the agendas of their respective legislative bodies. It is, for example, much easier for the president than it is for a member of Congress, let alone for you or me, to get the attention of Congress on a particular matter. Or ask any member of a city council whether it is easier for a council member or for the mayor to persuade council to consider a proposal for action. In most situations, the mayor is the winner.

2. What is the general climate of opinion at the time a particular policy is proposed? That is, what do people seem to be concerned about? The history of the rights of minority groups is replete with examples of abuses which were at one particular moment of history not a matter of concern to the general public. They were ideas whose time had not yet come. In this latter half of the 20th century it is difficult even to comprehend that in the early part of this century women (in Massachusetts, for example) were imprisoned for up to two years for the crimes of stub-

bornness, disorderly or lewd behavior, nightwalking, or adultery. Thus do policy agendas change as public attitudes change.

3. What is the attitude of the media toward the proposed policy? It is not enough to ask if the media support or oppose an idea. One must ask if they even care about it. Obviously, the media do not operate in a vacuum. At times they may lead, at other times they may only mirror public attitudes. It seems that the media have an impact only when their statements strike a sympathetic chord with the general public. Media publicity about the abuse of women was not particularly newsworthy early in the 20th century; it became news late in this century. One may wonder if the now acceptable use of animals for research purposes might not be reconsidered at some time in the future as more is learned about animals and their feelings. Will the media lead public attitudes on this topic, will it be content to follow, or will it not consider the topic newsworthy? As you, the student, read this, ask yourself if this topic deserves to be on the policy agenda.

4. Has one of the major political parties identified the topic as worthy of its attention? Are key members of Congress or a state legislature espousing a particular policy? While it is true that presidents generally are better able to get their favorite topics ''on the table'' for public discussion than are members of Congress, the latter are not totally without influence or support, and in some cases the support comes in the form of influential interest groups.

5. Is there some evidence of a perceived crisis? Strengthening legislation regulating the purity and safety of food, drugs, and cosmetics has on more than one occasion been given a boost by a crisis, just as spending for the military tends to reflect changes in public attitudes and the public's fear of foreign powers as a result of perceived threats to American security.

While the preceding list does not exhaust all possible questions one might ask, if the answers to the listed questions are affirmative, then it is likely that the topic will make it to the policy agenda.

The next stage in the policy process is referred to as policy formulation. A summarized description of this stage will be sufficient for our purposes. First, it should be noted that many of the same actors described earlier will be involved: governmental officials, legislators, interest groups, the media, interested citizens. The goal in this stage will be to identify the compromises which have enough support to gain some kind of consensus. At least that is the goal in most cases. For example, in the 1930's, those supporting the strengthening of the food and drug laws were determined to eliminate false advertising by giving regulatory control to the Food and Drug Administration, rather than to the Federal Trade Commission. The reason behind this goal was to force advertisers to be subject to the possibility of fines and imprisonment (FDA powers), rather than the relatively impotent "cease and desist" powers of the FTC. Both regulatory agencies had friends in Congress, and the proposed law languished and died in congressional conference committee on the issue of control of advertising. Hostility toward the advertising industry in those years by some groups in our society was so intense that compromise seemed impossible. When in 1937 a crisis intervened (the deaths of over 100 people, many of them children) and revived the demand for strengthened laws, Congress responded to the thorny issue by separating labeling from advertising. Control of labeling went to the FDA, advertising to the FTC. What is clear is that from 1932 until 1938, the failure to approve a policy was the acceptable "policy." However, it should be noted that the consensus thus achieved was *not* a victory for the enemies of advertising (enemies which included key officials of the administration of President Roosevelt); rather, it was an acceptance by them of their inability to win. It is impossible to know whether the policy thus formulated represented majority views, but it did represent the consensus of the key actors involved in the decision-making process; and that is the point to keep in mind. While the example used here has been the passage of an act of Congress, we could just as easily have described a state legislature struggling over the passage of a state law, a city council dealing with a city ordinance, a government agency creating a regulation, or a group of citizens attempting to gain approval of a referendum. In each of these arenas the process of policy formulation is basically the same. While the goal is to gain approval of a policy, that approval may be long delayed (as in the case of the food and drug laws), or it may never occur. Nonaction represents a type of decision just as surely as does action.

When the policy formulation stage has been completed the policy has become "legitimated," meaning it is ready to be implemented. Perhaps this will mean that an agency must be established to enforce the policy, funds appropriated to pay for the enforcement, or procedures established to carry out the mandate created by the policy.

Here then, we have an overview of the policy process. In the simulation which follows there is a focus on one segment of the policy process, the decision-making or "policy and program formulation and legitimation" stage. Both the initiation stage and agenda-setting stage are givens for our purposes. As will be explained later, it is assumed that they are already complete. In addition, the last stage of the policy process, implementation, will not be involved.

To prepare for the simulation, you will need to be introduced to three seemingly disparate topics: (1) interest groups, (2) eminent domain, and (3) a case study of an actual event. All three topics, you will discover, are essential to your understanding of the lessons of the simulation.

First, let us look at interest groups, which we have identified as one of the essential actors in the policy formulation stage of the policy process. Our objective will be to review briefly what interest groups are and what factors seem to influence their effectiveness.

Interest Groups: Characteristics and Factors Influencing Effectiveness

Interest groups come in many shapes and forms, and there have been numerous attempts to define, categorize, and classify them. Scholars are divided on the subject. Some argue that any collection of people trying to achieve some political objective is an interest group, but that definition is broad enough to include political parties. What if one of the bureaucracies tries to get something for itself (for example, the army wants more tanks, the police want more police), are these agencies then interest groups? Or, if a school board campaigns for a school tax levy, is it an interest group? Perhaps the answer is who knows? Or even, who cares? We as scholars trying to understand and measure the influence of interest groups care, simply because we must define something before we can measure its influence. But perhaps we don't have to be too concerned about the precision of the definition. Any group of persons trying to gain some *political* objective is assumed to be an interest group. Note the adjective *political* in our definition. We are concerned about the political process, not social, educational, religious, economic, or other processes; and our focus, therefore, is on attempts to influence political decision makers, whether they be national, state, or local.

Don't be confused by the fact that European scholars tend to use the phrase *pressure groups* while *interest groups* is the more commonly used expression among American scholars. Both terms refer to the same thing. Some interest groups are highly organized (such as the National Association of Manufacturers or the National Education Association), others are loosely organized (such as the women's liberation movement). There are very large and very small groups, very rich and very poor, very influential and not very influential. In addition, interest groups may be organized on an economic basis to protect a particular industry (farm price supports or tariffs on Japanese automobiles); on a social basis to protect particular people (assistance for battered wives, housing for the elderly); on an ideological basis (anything from prayers in public schools to socialism); and on and on. There is no need to elaborate these differences here, but there are characteristics we should understand, such as (1) the most important factors which determine the effectiveness of an interest group, and (2) possible differences between interest groups at the national level and those at the local level.

Contrary to the belief of many people, interest group conflict is not a struggle of good versus evil. Much of our experience, especially in our youth, portrays life as if it were a struggle of good people trying to succeed against all the obstacles put in their way, rather like an arcade computer game or a *Star Wars* movie. Thus we often carry these images to our observations of interest group conflict, causing us to wonder why decision makers vote as they do. Sometimes, when they fail to agree with our position, we accuse them of being "politicians" (whatever that means), or "selling out to powerful interests." In fact, unlike the typical computer game which pits good against evil, interest group conflict involves several different factors and dimensions which affect political outcomes.

The first of these factors is the particular issue. Is it narrow, very specific in its appeal and goals, or is it broad gauge? As a general rule, the narrower the objective an issue has, the better its chance of success. The National Rifle Association, for example, has a very narrow goal: opposition to gun control. Contrast that with groups whose objective is to "protect the environment." Not surprisingly, the NRA has a much clearer record of protecting its interests.

A second factor is the interest group itself. Just as narrower objectives generally are easier to achieve than broad-gauged ones, so also can smaller groups focus their resources more effectively. A good rule to remember is that the larger the group, the greater the diversity of membership and thus the greater the difficulty in gaining consensus. The opposite is true for small groups, hence their advantage.

Another factor which seems to have an impact on the conflict among interest groups is how strongly the members of a group feel about an issue. The term used to express this is intensity. Compare, for example, the position of the Catholic Church and many Catholics on the issue of abortion with their attitudes toward labor legislation. The abortion issue is hardly a casual one to them; it is in fact something which is so intensely felt that it may crowd out all other public policy issues from their agenda. Labor legislation, on the other hand, may be important, but it does not evoke the intensity of feeling produced by the abortion issue. Now look at the other side of the coin. Organized labor views right-to-work laws as another name for "union busting" and will fight tenaciously against these proposals, which outlaw union shops and permit the employment of non-union workers who need not join a union to remain employed. The AFL-CIO will do everything in its power to prevent the passage of such laws, mobilizing its members to send telegrams and write letters to legislators, sending its lobbyists to persuade legislators (or threaten them with defeat at the next election). Conversely, it is highly unlikely that an organization as diverse in its membership as the

AFL-CIO will feel intensely about the abortion issue, even though some members may.

This brings us to the factors which influence decision makers: (a) access, (b) the salience (that is, the perceived importance) of the issue, and (c) accurate, useful information. Put yourself in the position of a member of Congress, state legislator, or city council member. Are you going to be impressed by how large an organization is? Or by how many telegrams you receive? Perhaps. But social science research tells us that of far more importance is whether a particular group has unusual access to you. If that particular group has access, then it makes little difference how small or large the group is. Access can refer to the greater ability of your friends and neighbors to influence your vote in city council as contrasted to the position of strangers, or it can mean that you are likely to listen carefully and give due regard to a well-organized, powerful group in your district, city, or state which is critical to your reelection. If you are a member of Congress who represents Flint, Michigan, it is very likely that your door will be open to the United Auto Workers and their representatives, and their concerns are very likely your concerns.

The second factor of importance to you as a decision maker is salience, meaning just how important is this issue to you. It may be important because it coincides with your own values. For example, you may not be Catholic, but if in principle you oppose abortion, then the "Right to Life" issue is very salient and the anti-abortion position of the Catholic Church will be viewed very sympathetically. It may also be true that on a particular issue you personally have no strong feelings. However, if many or most of your constituents think an issue is important, you may come to feel the issue is salient because your constituents do.

Third, and perhaps most important of all as a factor influencing decisions, is useful and accurate information. You, as a decision maker, constantly have to deal with complex and highly technical topics. Even at the local level, the decisions you will be asked to make will require a level of knowledge and expertise far beyond that of the average citizen who runs for office. Thus decision makers have to depend on measurable information and expert opinion. And that is what many interest groups do particularly well. They provide accurate, useful information. Quantifiable data are especially helpful in these situations. Representatives of these groups try to provide information that will pull the minds of decision makers their way.

So it is that the most effective interest groups will be those (1) which have the best access to decision makers, (2) whose issues are most salient to the decision maker, (3) who have taken a stand which makes the issue salient, and (4) whose information or expertise is particularly helpful to the decision maker in deciding how to vote on an issue, and, perhaps equally important, how to explain that vote to the public.

Are the interest groups which deal with Congress or state legislatures the same as those which try to influence a city council? For the most part, no. In the first place, the scale of projects at the federal level is enormous, while that of most cities is small. Most of the largest interest groups will simply not have much interest in what goes on at the local level. But there are exceptions. Some ideological groups will be organized down to the grass roots level and will attempt to influence all levels of decision making. ''Right to Life'' representatives, for example, can be found testifying in favor of a proposed city ordinance restricting the activities of city abortion clinics or at congressional hearings on proposed legislation to prohibit tax money use to pay for abortions. Some large corporations likewise may at times be found testifying at all levels. For example, gas and electric companies have a stake in local rate franchises granted by city councils as well as in proposed regulatory legislation at the state and national levels.

However, at the local level it is far more likely that the interest groups will be ad hoc, meaning they appear suddenly in response to an emerging issue and then disappear when the issue is resolved. An example would be a fast food chain which asks permission of city council to change the zoning restrictions so that a restaurant can be built in an area zoned for single family houses. This evokes an angry response from the people in the surrounding neighborhood, who then circulate petitions and appear at council meetings to oppose the rezoning. Council deliberates, listens carefully to the outraged citizens—who are not only voters but perhaps also neighbors and friends of members of city council— and decides against the restaurant chain. The angry citizens then calm down and return to their own concerns. The interest group disappears. This is the typical history of an ad hoc interest group. It is a common phenomenon at the local level. At the state or national level, the appearance of an ad hoc group is far less prevalent. Think of the modal patterns of interest groups as a spectrum, with ad hoc groups as one end and full-time, paid professional lobbyists as the other end. With that spectrum in mind, the mode at the local level is ad hoc, while the mode at the national level is that of full-time, paid professionals. At the state level, the mode is one of part-time lobbyists who are full-time at something else. University officials, for example, often are required to spend considerable time at the state capitol when the legislature is in session, attempting to convince legislators of the necessity to increase subsidy for the state universities. Yet these university officials are not paid lobbyists, for their full-time positions are typically that of university president, or treasurer, or perhaps a faculty member who happens to be president of a faculty senate.

In order to illustrate the role of interest groups in the decision-making process and their impact on decision makers, this simulation introduces a problem which has become increasingly common, especially in northern cities—the threat of an industry to leave the city. Often this threat spurs a city council to action. What can the city council do to persuade the company to stay, for the loss of a large corporation means not only the loss of jobs for the citizens of the city and the loss of tax income to pay for essential services, it also means that at the same time some expenses will increase dramatically to meet the needs of those who will be rendered jobless. An industry may leave, but most of its people stay and try to find new jobs.

In an effort to keep industries from leaving, some cities have lent their eminent domain power (the right of government to take private property for public use with just compensation) to industry. Or, as in the case to be described, a city may use the eminent domain authority itself in order to meet the stated needs of an industry. Since industry usually does not have eminent domain power, the city's use of the power in this way has the potential of enabling an industry to assemble parcels of land which otherwise would not be for sale.

In the pages to follow you will encounter an introduction to the concept of eminent domain and a description of some of its newer uses. Then a case history is provided of an event in Atlantis (based on an actual event in the United States, when Detroit sought to keep a General Motors plant in the city). You will discover for yourself what it is like to be thrust into a conflict among interest groups, particularly ad hoc interest groups. What should decision makers do when the choice must be made between people who need jobs and people who need their homes?

The Newer Uses of the Power of Eminent Domain

The Fifth Amendment of the U.S. Constitution is about due process; it describes the procedures which the national government must follow before any person can be deprived of life, liberty, or property. One clause of that Amendment states, ". . . nor shall private property be taken for public use, without just compensation." Referred to commonly as the "eminent domain clause," these seemingly straightforward words conceal remarkable patterns of complexity, rich in their imprecision. It is almost as if every other word were a swamp full of quicksand. What does "property" mean, and in particular "private property"? Is it only pieces of real estate, land and building? What is "public use"? Are privately owned railroads public use? Could an automobile manufacturing plant ever be considered public use? A professional football team? And what is "just compensation"? Does it always have to be paid? Everyone would agree that if the state builds a road through your property it will pay you for the land. But what if property is not taken but instead is restricted severely in its use? This clearly was the case when the 18th Amendment was ratified in 1919, and the resulting congressional enforcement law forbade the manufacture, distribution, and sale of alcoholic beverages. The companies which made the products were faced with the obligation to destroy warehouses full of aging bourbon, brandy, and other whiskies. Wineries everywhere went bankrupt, the vineyards sometimes sold to pay back taxes. This was clearly an example of private property being burdened (its use constrained) in furtherance of a governmental policy; but there was no compensation, for there had been no "taking" of property by the government for a public purpose.

State constitutions generally contain something similar to the

U.S. Constitution concerning the taking of private property, in some instances stating clearly what kinds of things can or cannot be taken via eminent domain. State legislatures and constitutions have gone one step further and have delegated the power of eminent domain to local governments and also to certain private corporations, typically utilities such as railroads, gas and electric power, telephone, and water. The assumption is that these utilities are necessary and must be granted eminent domain authority in order to carry out essential functions. The nature of their operations requires them to acquire thin, linear tracts of land or right-of-way permissions in order to receive and distribute their service to the public. A stubborn landowner or two, unwilling to sell or willing to sell only at an exorbitant price, could prevent the utility's development. Eminent domain authority avoids such a stalemate.

Ordinarily, other private businesses have not been granted such power since it is generally accepted that, while their activities are presumably useful to society, the services of any one company are not essential. Moreover, it has not been thought that such a business had a compelling need for one particular piece of land; alternative locations could be found to serve the business just about as effectively. However, today the answer to who shall be granted eminent domain power is in the process of change through expansion.

A startling example of how much the concept has changed was reported in the *Washington Post* on June 22, 1982 (page D-2). Announced was a decision of the California Supreme Court "that the city of Oakland (California) has the right to acquire the Oakland Raiders professional football franchise under its power of eminent domain." The court, by a 6-1 vote, stated:

> The acquisition and, indeed, the operation of a sports franchise may well be an appropriate function. That being so, the statutes discussed herein afford the city the power to acquire by eminent domain any property necessary to carry out that function.

What is not always understood by the public is that the eminent domain clause does not require the government to compensate you in every situation when property is taken or denied. For example, every time taxes are raised, the government takes property from you, in this case the property is income. When price controls, wage controls, or credit controls are imposed, property is denied you. In every one of these examples, the government has decreed that you must give up something of value—a portion of your income, typically. And in none of these instances is there any compensation. Think how farmers must feel when they must pay more for seed, fertilizer, and gasoline, yet because of price controls cannot raise the price of agricultural produce! Who compensates wage earners when wage controls are invoked? Or suppose property taxes are so high that a business goes bankrupt. Ridiculous, you say? Then what about farmers whose land has been encroached upon by suburbia to the extent that it is zoned and taxed as land available for housing or commercial development? There are well-documented instances of a tax bill demanding more than fifteen times the preceding year's tax on the same farm land. Where does the farmer whose taxes jumped from $2,000 to $34,000 get the cash to pay? Suddenly the farmer-landowner has to pay such high real estate taxes that farming is no longer financially feasible. The final irony for the farmer is that if the housing boom stops because of a recession, the land may be unsellable, but the taxes have to be paid anyhow. The farmer may then face the worst of all possibilities: ownership of land which cannot be sold because of the end of a land boom, but taxes so high that sale of farm products will not cover all expenses. Even if the farmer decides to let the land lie fallow, this will not help, for the taxes must be paid. If they are not, the county government will place a lien on the land and order the sheriff to auction off the land to pay the taxes. So much for "just compensation."

Or let us say that you bought or inherited a lovely old building. The local taxes are very high, and you decide that the only way you can pay the taxes is to modify the building so as to create rental apartments. An interesting surprise may await you: the zoning laws may not permit the conversion. There is also the possibility that your building will be designated a "historic landmark" and in some states that may mean the government will tell you what you must do to maintain the property and how you may use it! You may even be denied the right to make changes in the structure, changes which would enable you to make enough income to cover the costs of ownership. The famous case involving the Grand Central Terminal in New York was just such an example. The City of New York felt that this famous architectural wonder must be preserved as it was for the enjoyment of tourists and local citizens. The Penn Central Railroad was the unfortunate owner prevented from modifying the building to increase rental income.

In the United States the arbiter of every one of the disputes is the courts. It is they who decide if the property can be taken, if the use is indeed permissible under the federal or state constitution, if compensation is to be paid, and if so, how much.

Now let us turn our attention to an actual decision-making situation in Detroit, Michigan.

Interests and Actors in the Policy Process: A Case Study

The events and the actors in the simulation are drawn from real events in Detroit, Michigan. It may be useful to learn some of the details of those events for they will reveal several points, including the role played by the different actors (the mayor and the interest groups), the newer uses of eminent domain, and an example of the painful dilemma stated in our title, needs and rights in collision.

Early in 1980, the General Motors Corporation announced that it was closing its automobile assembly plant in St. Louis and moving to the suburban fringe. Thus came to an end 60 years of a relationship whereby GM provided jobs in St. Louis for 10,000 workers (10% of the work force) and $200 million in annual tax revenues, while the city provided the essential services (police, fire protection, street maintenance, and so on).

The announcement was especially surprising and infuriating to officials because it came on the heels of an earlier announcement that GM was planning to invest $100 million in expansion and renovation of the existing plant. St. Louis public officials had worked eagerly to meet GM's stated need for additional land by allocating $2 million of public funds to buy acreage adjacent to the plant. The mayor and council believed they were doing just what GM wanted them to do by showing St. Louis' commitment to its largest employer.

The General Motors Corporation decision to leave St. Louis was not the heartless act of unfeeling company officials. It was, rather, the result of many factors—including a physical plant which had lost its usefulness at least 20 years earlier as a result of changing technologies and a city so built-up that no tract of open land of the needed size was available. To find the required 400 acres in the city of St. Louis would result in massive disruption, relocation, and scattering of hundreds of people and dozens of businesses; it would destroy many communities, many neighborhoods. No tract of land acceptable to General Motors could be located. In many ways the company was fighting for its own existence. Foreign competition was eating away at GM's share of the market, and if it was to survive and be able to compete successfully over the next several decades, then new and efficient plants would have to be built. GM officials feared that if they started to worry about saving cities, rather than about building automobiles, they might not be able to do either.

Although GM officials gave the impression that they were little concerned about the St. Louis episode, in reality the adverse publicity was troublesome. Therefore when the company announced in June 1980 the closing of two obsolete Detroit plants, it included a statement to the effect that a new plant would be built within the city limits of Detroit if a suitable site could be found. Detroit Mayor Coleman Young, after a review of possible locations, offered to GM a 465-acre tract that included Dodge Main, a huge old Chrysler plant closed 15 months earlier. However, there was one unfortunate aspect of the Coleman proposal: included in the 465 acres was a 250 acre section known familiarly as Poletown. Here existed a Polish-American community of long standing which now faced the prospect of some 3,400 people being forced to move to make way for the plant. Although the homes were old and of modest size, this was not a slum district with crumbling foundations, rats, and abandoned buildings. It was, in fact, a genuine community, almost half of whose members were elderly. The bulldozers would wipe out 1,500 private homes, plus schools, businesses, and 16 churches. The potential for human agony was clear.

There was yet another aspect of the problem which was even more galling to some of the residents. Mayor Young took advantage of a recently approved Michigan "quick take" law, which allowed a city to use its eminent domain powers to acquire land and properties for use by private enterprise. The "quick take" law contained one fascinating provision: owners of the property so acquired had to be off the land within 60 days! Whereas the typical eminent domain laws do not permit governmental entry onto the land until just compensation has been established and paid, this new law limited the court's role to settling disputes over the amount to be paid for the property. The owner could not postpone the date of acquisition by litigating the amount to be paid! In other words, 60 days after the city made its decision to buy your property, the bulldozers could be at work, even if you were still protesting that you were not being adequately reimbursed. Under the "quick take" procedure, negotiation over the amount, including possible court review, had been separated from acquisition. To illustrate the problem, how persuasive do you think you could be in describing to a jury the former value of a home now reduced to rubble? Wouldn't you rather show them the structure intact?

The agony faced by Poletown residents was not a simple matter of a faceless, uncaring corporation destroying good American neighborhoods, uprooting families, crushing churches. At stake also was the future of the city of Detroit, for GM promised employment of a minimum of 3,000 people for one shift in the new plant. If the cars sold well, a second shift of an additional 3,000 people would be hired. To hard-pressed Mayor Young this trade-off was painful, but it had to be. As with other northern cities of the "smokestack" era, Detroit was indeed a sick city. The new $500-million GM plant held the prospect of employing 6,000 workers and adding some $8 million a year in tax revenues. Some must suffer so that many more will benefit: the classic confrontation of individual rights versus community needs.

Equally important in the thinking of Detroit city officials was their belief that the property owners were being offered very good prices, often twice what these aged properties would obtain on the open market, plus generous resettlement benefits to both owners and renters. In addition, the city purchased federally owned housing units for the Poletowners and offered them mortgages at a bargain rate of 9.5% interest.

The Mayor obviously had many supporters. Labor leaders praised the city officials for this effort to bring jobs to Detroit. The

Detroit Coalition of Black Trade Unionists supported the city efforts.

But what about those who were to be uprooted, some of whom
have lived their entire life in this neighborhood, in this home. The
Catholic priest, whose parish would be scattered to the winds,
would watch the walls of his church crumble. The Poletown
Neighborhood Council was formed to fight the bureaucrats. Lawyers were hired, and a suit was filed in Federal District Court to
block the plant. Ralph Nader joined the fight. Their demand was
simple: find another site. This heartless company, in their view,
had no right to destroy this community of 3,400 people. The Poletown Council contended that great pressure had been applied by
city appraisers to persuade those who had already accepted the
city's offer. This was not "due process," claimed the opponents.
It was a forced sale. Would they leave? Some of the residents said
"under no circumstances." Some even threatened violence. Others merely wept. To be told to be out of their homes within 60 days
of the notice was truly a cruel fate.

As in our simulation, you will note that Detroit Mayor Coleman
Young was heavily influenced by the earlier events which occurred in St. Louis. Thus the initiation stage of the policy process
really began prior to the events in Detroit. In order to understand
the policy process, one cannot ignore the circumstances which
preceded current efforts to formulate a policy. For Detroit Mayor
Young, the initiation stage began in St. Louis in 1980. And thus
the threat of a repetition of the St. Louis events occurring in Detroit in 1981 stimulated Mayor Young to place his proposed policy on the public agenda. And it was at the policy formulation
stage of the policy process, that is, when the Detroit City Council
considered Mayor Young's plan, that the interest group struggle
really began. The General Motors Corporation was, insofar as can
be determined by newspaper coverage of the issue, outside the
process. They had laid down their conditions for staying in the
City of Detroit.

Now it is your turn. The City Council of Alpha City, you will
discover, must deal with a situation similar to that in Detroit. At
issue are rights and needs in collision. Whose should prevail,
those of the larger community or those of the residents of the
threatened neighborhood? What would you decide if you were a
member of the city council?

The Simulation

Situated on the shores of Mirror Lake, Alpha City is one of the de-
caying Alpha cities which flourished when heavy industry was
king. Today, while its suburbs are flourishing, the central city is
not. In the last decade Alpha City has lost 30% of its population
with the flight of both industry and people to the suburbs and to
the cities of Beta. Thus the central city has suffered and continues
to suffer the loss of tax revenues and employment opportunities.
More than this, the city has had to bear the burden of steadily increasing welfare costs while at the same time experiencing declining revenues from property and income taxes as industries
shut down or moved. A huge manufacturing plant in the industrial basin area of the city lies abandoned, a museum piece from
another era, too obsolete to be utilized, too costly to be removed.
Old automobile assembly plants, several stories high, sit crumbling, or partially used as ill-suited warehouses or for marginal
industries seeking low cost quarters.

Surrounding this area of industrial decay are neighborhoods of
working class homes built decades ago. They continue to house
people who remain, some for reasons of loyalty to their traditional
ethnic neighborhoods and places of worship. Thus one area is
known affectionately as Little Warsaw and another as Little Na-
ples, and so on. A newer group, the Omegans, has been growing
rapidly, and they too have tended to cluster together. Like St.
Louis and Detroit in the United States, Alpha City is declining.
Over the past ten years it has been losing people and industry as
steadily as sand drains out of an hour glass.

The Fact Sheet on page 71 provides additional information
about various aspects of the employment situation in Alpha City.

Two years ago the people of Alpha City elected the first Omegan ever to be mayor, a very able, forceful, articulate, and extremely energetic attorney. He has worked ceaselessly to preach
the virtues of Alpha City, its rail and highway facilities, its un-
limited supplies of skilled labor and water, and its strategic location in the industrial center of Alpha. Primarily as a result of the
Mayor's efforts and the support he has gained from both the commercial and banking interests, Alpha City has begun to stir. Old
buildings are being razed and phoenixlike glistening high rises

are beginning to rise from the ashes of abandoned sites. Now comes the most ambitious plan of all. The Mayor has learned that the Atlantis United Corporation plans to build a new vehicle assembly plant and has announced the closing of its fifty-year-old Alpha City plant. The new plant is planned for Beta. Alpha City's mayor is fighting back, however. He has proposed to Atlantis United a package of incentives consisting of Atlantis government funds (already approved) to purchase homes, stores, churches, and industries in the area and locally sponsored industrial revenue bonds to relocate and build the access highways and rail connections. The Mayor's plan also includes property tax concessions. One aspect has not yet been settled. Here is the problem.

The Atlantis United Corporation has located the site it wants and has indicated its unwillingness to compromise on this point. In order to build a modern assembly plant, it requires 500 acres of land. Since it already has acquired the land in Beta, Atlantis United has stated that it sees no purpose in discussing a package which is less than satisfactory for its needs. If it is to stay in Alpha City, the specified acreage and its location are not negotiable items. While the Mayor is in full agreement, the human cost for the inhabitants of Alpha City is going to be high if council approves the plan.

No one has complained about the financial aspects of the plan, other than the critic of big business, who views the entire plan as a disgraceful public "giveaway" to an arrogant company. He is particularly upset with the "we won't negotiate" attitude of the company. The plan calls for generous payments to the property owners, plus relocation grants to all the home owners and businesses in the area. What has really upset the people of the area is that council is being asked to use its eminent domain power to take private property, the result being that the residents (according to provincial law) will be removed within 60 days. The home and business owners, if council approves the plan, will have no opportunity to agree, disagree, or negotiate. The bulldozers will be on the site in 60 days. If the property owners do not like the price being offered or the relocation arrangements they can of course take the matter to court. But they cannot prevent the acquisition of the property nor delay the razing of the structures.

Of course, many of the members of the neighborhood marked for destruction are furious and afraid, furious about the possibility of forced and immediate destruction of their community and their churches and afraid of an uncertain future in which they must seek satisfactory replacement housing.

Yet the problem is not a simple one. As the Mayor points out again and again, unemployment is high in Alpha City and especially in the Omegan community. If Atlantis United leaves, another 2,000 jobs will move out of the city. Thus even more unemployment is guaranteed. But if the new and expanded vehicle assembly plant can be built, then a single shift will provide 2,500 jobs and Atlantis United has assured the city that there will be at least one shift in operation. If demand increases and a second shift is needed, then there is the possibility of 5,000 jobs. Surely, says the Mayor, it is reasonable to ask about 1,000 people to make a sacrifice, which involves no financial loss to them and perhaps a gain, so that many more will have jobs. What is more, the assembly plant will spawn many other support and service industries, which will generate more jobs and more income for the city. Tax revenues, not welfare costs, will increase.

There is an additional plus for the city if the plant is built. What economists refer to as the multiplier effect will be at work. If 2,500 workers are employed, then it is estimated that for each dollar they spend, this will be multiplied by $2\frac{1}{2}$, as their spending ripples through the local economy. What is more, the other social costs referred to above will be lessened as men and women engage in productive work and enjoy the psychological benefits of feeling that they are again useful citizens and valuable human beings.

All this is little solace for the neighborhood. As the role descriptions will reveal, the neighborhood remains unconvinced. They are the ones being asked to sacrifice their homes, their community, their lifelong friendships, and their church. The benefits will go chiefly to others.

There you have the problem and the issue: Shall eminent domain authority be used to take private property for corporate use?

When community needs (building a new assembly plant to reduce unemployment and raise tax revenues) conflict with individual property rights, which should prevail? How do you decide when community needs are paramount? What criteria should be used?

Stage One: The Setting

The simulation which follows is a meeting of the Alpha City Council. At this meeting, the following proposed ordinance is the only issue on the agenda:

> "Be it resolved: The City of Alpha is herewith authorized to use its powers of eminent domain to condemn and purchase the 500-acre tract as described in the proposal of the Atlantis United Corporation."

Council members will seat themselves in a row in front of the class. The Mayor will be seated in the middle of the members of council. The Mayor will preside over the council meeting and may not vote, except to break a tie. Members of council and all individuals in the audience must be recognized by the Mayor before being allowed to speak. All remarks by members of the audience must be directed to council and not to other members of the audience.

Stage Two: Running the Simulation

NOTE: A brief explanation of the principles of Parliamentary Procedure is located in the Appendix. You will find especially useful for reference during the simulation run the Rank Order of Commonly Used Motions (p. 219) and the Sequence of Motions chart (p. 219).

The Roles

NOTE: These are very angry individuals. Those who play these roles should plan to take very assertive positions.

The Neighborhood Representatives

1. Older woman (a widow). Has lived since her marriage in a house which will be destroyed.

2. Daughter of widow. Lived all her life in the same house. Sees

that the loss will include a neighborhood community as well as just a house.

3. Belligerent man. Does not want money for house, does not want to leave the neighborhood and the community. "I'll shoot anyone who tries to make me move."

4. Retired man. Just retired and also celebrated his 50th wedding anniversary. He and his wife have lived all their married life in the house which has been marked for destruction.

5. Wife of #4. Worries about the effect on her husband of the razing of the house. She has a heart condition and has been upset by her husband's recent retirement and now she is almost in despair at the thought of having to find a new home.

6. Machinist. Has not been able to find steady work but has been able to survive because the cost of maintenance on his modest home has been minimal. Now he must find a new home, which will very likely cost much more. In addition, he will be forced to commute long distances to any job.

7. Young attorney. Grew up in the area and now lives at home with parents while getting started in a law practice. Is very angry because the neighborhood will be destroyed.

8. Elementary school teacher. Also grew up in the area. Had always wanted to return to the area to teach. Now both home and school will be destroyed. Will be forced to find a new home and then commute to a school far removed from old friends and the new home.

9. Priest. His church will be torn down. The loss will be his entire life, a congregation scattered, a viable community destroyed, people he loves hurt.

10. Assistant to the Priest. While he is new to this parish, it has always seemed ideal to him because of the loyalty and devotion of the parishioners to each other and to the church.

The Larger Community Representatives

NOTE: These individuals will *not* use an angry style of presentation. They will attempt to persuade the city council by emphasizing the goals and needs of the larger community.

11. An Omegan civic leader. He sees the employment possibilities for his people if the new plant is built, lessening the very serious unemployment.

12. The Mayor (see earlier discussion).

13. The neighborhood retailer. Business will not be destroyed. Sees growth and change as a positive factor. The new plant will help the business by providing employment for many customers. Will make the entire area more prosperous and thus help the entire city.

14. The labor leader. Has watched the impact of all the plant closing on the union local. Sees a revived industrial base as the source of growth and strength for the union and for the newer residents of the city, the Omegans.

The Outside Critic

NOTE: His or her presentation will also be angry. Emphasis will be antibusiness and attempt to make the corporation the enemy.

15. National spokesperson of a consumer organization, a critic of big business and of corporate practices. Is particularly hostile to the Atlantis United Corporation, whose arrogance in the past was responsible for the national recognition this consumer organization gained.

The Decision Makers

16. Member of Council #1

17. Member of Council #2

18. Member of Council #3

19. Member of Council #4

20. Member of Council #5

21. Member of Council #6

22. Member of Council #7

NOTE: Council members at an appropriate time will avail themselves of the opportunity to ask questions.

The Public Hearing

The first part of the session will be a public hearing. The following procedure will be used.
   The Mayor will state:

"Council will please come to order. This is a public hearing on the question of whether eminent domain powers shall be granted to the Atlantis United Corporation for the purpose of acquiring the necessary land to build a new truck assembly plant. Those who favor the granting of eminent domain will now be given an opportunity to speak. All comments will be directed to council. No person will be permitted to speak unless that individual has been recognized by me. Who wishes to speak in support of the granting of eminent domain?"

For additional information about various aspects of the employment situation in Alpha City, refer to the Alpha City Fact Sheet on p. 71.

The Mayor will then recognize one at a time all those who favor granting eminent domain to the Atlantis United Corporation.
   When all those favoring the granting of eminent domain have had an opportunity to speak, the Mayor will then state:

"Those who oppose the granting of eminent domain to the Atlantis United Corporation will now be given an opportunity to speak. Again let me remind you that all comments will be directed to council and not to any individual in the audience.

No person will be permitted to speak unless that individual has been recognized by me. Who wishes to speak in opposition to the granting of eminent domain?''

When all those opposing the granting of eminent domain have had an opportunity to speak, the Mayor will then state:

''Members of council will now be given an opportunity to ask questions of any member of the audience. Does any member wish to ask any questions?''

When council members have asked whatever questions they have, the Mayor will then state:

''Does any member of the audience wish to make any comment?''

The Meeting of Council

Following this, council members will be given an opportunity to debate the issue publicly among themselves.

NOTE: Except for those members of the class who have been assigned to specific roles, you may play yourself, a citizen of Alpha. Members of council may also play themselves.

Council must come to a decision. (NOTE: Even a nondecision is a decision.)

Stage Three: Debriefing and Critique ————

At a time designated by your instructor, the simulation will be ended and the debriefing and critique will take place.

NOTE: Your instructor may ask you to complete and turn in the evaluation form on the page following the Alpha City Fact Sheet.

1. James E. Anderson, *Public Policy Making*, 2nd ed. (Boston: Holt, Rinehart, and Winston, 1979) p. 3.
2. Ibid., p. 55.

Alpha City Fact Sheet

No attempt has been made to provide every possible piece of factual information. However, included here are the most relevant pieces of information you may need.

Population of the metropolitan area:	1,539,387
Number eligible for employment (est. 50%)	769,693
Number employed as of last month	655,779
Number unemployed as of last month (14.8%)	113,914

Unemployed by ethnic group:	
Caucasian (13.4%)	66,042
Southeast Asian (Omegan) (32%)	41,970
All other (18%)	5,902
Total unemployed	113,914

Ethnic composition of employed:	
Caucasian (75%)	491,834
Southeast Asian (Omegan) (20%)	131,156
Hispanic (3%)	19,673
Other (2%)	13,116
Total employed	655,779

Number employed currently engaged in manufacturing (15 years old and older) (30.9%)	202,636
Number of people aged 1–15 (23.9%)	367,913

Jobs to be added by the new plant: 2,500 guaranteed; 6,000 possible.

Evaluation Form **Simulation Three**

1. In comparison with other courses, or portions of courses, which you have taken, how would you rate this simulation experience?

2. What do you consider to be the most important thing (or things) you learned from the simulation?

3. Was there anything about the simulation which you found disappointing?

4. Do you have any suggestions as to how the simulation might be improved?

5. Suppose a friend had a choice of introductory American Government sections, one of which used simulations such as the one you just experienced. The friend asks you whether he or she should choose the section offering the simulation. What would your advice be?

Please indicate whether your role was:
   _____ Very active member of council, or the mayor, or one of the involved citizens.
   _____ Moderately active (Spoke once or twice, but was not very involved.)
   _____ Slightly active (Active only within the delegation discussion.)
   _____ Inactive (Observed the events. Did not really participate in them.)

If more space is needed, the opposite side of this page may be used. If you wish to suggest changes or improvements in the simulation, please do so. Thank you.

Constituent Attitude Toward Representation

Trustee versus Instructed Delegate

Your representative owes you, not his industry only, but his judgment; and he betrays, instead of serving you, if he sacrifices it to your opinion.

Edmund Burke

Introduction

There is one constant theme which runs through most of the *Atlantis* simulations: You are presented with a situation involving conflict among one or more groups of individuals and your task is to deal with that conflict, struggling to see if you can resolve it, to find a satisfactory compromise.

This simulation differs from that pattern, for it does not build upon and develop intergroup conflict. Instead, it sets out to illustrate certain aspects of the process of representation, the relation of representatives to their constituencies, and some factors that tend to influence citizen evaluations of legislators. It does this by following a carefully constructed sequence of actions designed to illustrate the kinds of points mentioned above.

Theories of Representation

Before we get ourselves involved in a simulation, we need to explore some of our ideas on this subject of representation. Haven't we all, at some time or another, heard a friend say, "I vote for the best candidate, regardless of party"? But having heard such an assertion, how often do we stop to consider its full implication? How often do we stop and ask ourselves what did the friend mean by "the best"? How did our friend know that his or her vote had been cast for the best candidate?

Suppose that you decided to poll citizens in a shopping mall, asking them what qualities make up the best political candidate. The answers probably would cluster around such qualities as ability, experience, and honesty—qualities that are quite difficult to assess. But if we are to understand Atlantis, its problems, and its political processes, we need to probe more deeply than did the questions in the shopping mall; we need to probe more deeply this matter of ability. Ability to do what? In other words, we must identify the abilities which are relevant to the role of the public officer we are discussing. In order to make effective judgments as citizens we should have some notion of the responsibilities of the office. And if we are discussing present or prospective legislators, we must consider what is the proper relationship between the representative and his or her constituents.

One view of the proper relationship between the representative and the constituents is that the responsibility of the representative is to *pursue the wishes and preferences of the constituents*. Democracy, in this view, is promoted when the representative simply acts as a delegate, following the instructions of the folks back home. Perhaps you can recall watching a Republican or Democratic national convention in which delegates were bound to a particular candidate because the voters had chosen each delegate on the basis of the delegate's pledge to support that candidate. In fact, we usually call this theory of representation the "instructed delegate" theory (the label applies whether we are speaking of delegates to a convention or of senators in a state legislature). According to this theory, the duty of the representative is to mirror as faithfully and accurately as possible the wishes of the constituents. It is not much exaggerated to say that the model legislator, in this view, will "sit on a fence with an ear to the ground and a finger to the wind." An ungainly posture, to be sure, but one which helps the representative to gauge the temper of voter opinion and act in accordance with it, thus following the instructed delegate model. This instructed delegate model of behavior for representatives seems congruent with today's popular notions concerning democracy.

There is a contrasting, and older, theory of representation which has many proponents. In this contrasting view, the duty of a representative is to *act according to his or her own judgment on behalf of the best interests of the citizens,* in much the same way that trustees of a university act on behalf of the best interests of students, faculty, and the larger community. Another illustration is the board of trustees of a hospital, acting for the best interests of patients, staff, and the community. But notice the underlying question: Who determines what are "the best interests" of students, faculty, and the larger community? The answer, of course, is that the trustees themselves determine what is best for the clientele or constituency they are asked to protect. The trustee theory of representation calls for representatives to do what they consider best for their constituents.

Before he became president, John Kennedy wrote a book entitled *Profiles in Courage,* which called the reader's attention to the fateful and courageous actions of a series of individuals in public life. In each case, the individual took a stand which was contrary to the wishes of his constituency or to currently acceptable attitudes. Going counter to public opinion is not a good way to be popular or, in the case of these individuals, to keep your job. In each case, the individual felt that public opinion was wrong and acted contrary to that opinion. In several of John Kennedy's examples, the price paid for adhering to principle was defeat in election. Yet many times history has seemed to document the correctness of the stand taken by the person who believes in the trustee theory of representation, rather than that of the instructed delegate, who follows public opinion so slavishly.

Perhaps the ablest, and classic, statement of the trustee theory comes to us from Edmund Burke, a member of the British Parliament at the time of the American Revolution and for many years thereafter. In his "Address to the Electors of Bristol" (his constituency) Burke argues that the representative owes his best judgment to his constituents, whether that judgment agrees with theirs or not. As an aside we may note that his independence eventually cost him his seat in Parliament, but his argument remains and must be reckoned with even today, two centuries later.

Of course, any theory should be tested against available information to determine its value. What happens when we so test the instructed delegate theory and the trustee theory? How useful are these theories? How closely do they correspond to the world we observe and occupy? For example, there are several practical problems which you probably would encounter in attempting to follow the instructed delegate model. First of all, does a constituency actually have any preference on many of the legislative matters which come before Congress or before a state legislature? Does the constituency really have a judgment as to whether the rulemaking authority of the Food and Drug Administration should be exercised via notice and comment or via a trial-type proceeding on the record? Does the constituency really care whether judges of bankruptcy courts are paid the same salary as federal district court judges? These issues may well be important, but they are of such low salience to most people that it would be unrealistic to search for a constituency preference. Yet they must be settled by Congress one way or the other, for even inaction is a form of decision making.

A second practical problem arises from the difficulty of knowing (or determining) the constituency preferences even when a preference exists. How can we estimate constituency sentiments? Can a member of Congress talk to enough folks at county fairs and shopping malls to get a good feel for issues? Public opinion polling is quite costly—much too costly to be used routinely as a tool for the enhancement of democratic accountability on a district by district basis. Will letter writers to the representative comprise a cross-section of opinion? Can newspaper editors and editorials be depended upon for balanced views? What would you do as a representative?

A third difficulty encountered when one examines the instructed delegate model of representation is how the legislator handles the necessity for compromise. And where do political parties fit in? Is the model useful if it takes no account of parties? Or are parties irrelevant?

A fourth difficulty stems from the pace of development of legislative proposals. Is not the pace too fast for consultation with constituents to occur? Don't modifications and compromises emerge in ways and at times which require a prompt decision by the legislator?

Lastly, even if such consultation were possible, would it be useful and desirable? Aren't many matters of legislation rather complex for John Q. Public to absorb and evaluate in the time available after work and on weekends and by reading a newspaper and watching network news on TV? How much information can be found, even in the *New York Times* or in the *Washington Post,* concerning the wisdom of changing the income tax provisions relating to ''Subchapter S'' corporations? Even when the matter is more attentively considered by the news media, how much guidance may a Member of Congress expect from constituents regarding the relative merits of increasing our Trident missile capability in contrast to developing the MX missile? Moreover, is the Cruise missile an alternative or is it complementary to the others?

These are difficulties we encounter when we attempt to match our theories or models to reality.

By way of contrast, if we try to act upon the trustee theory, how tolerant will the voters be? Can a representative be wholly indifferent to constituency opinions and insist on acting according to his or her best judgment? And how does a matter such as the need for compromise during the legislative process relate to the trustee model? Does the trustee's "best judgment" include the possibility that best judgment may indicate the acceptance of compromise on the theory that half a loaf is indeed better than none? And how do political parties fit into this? Is there any place for parties if each representative has as his or her highest duty the obligation to see what is best for the constituents (conceding, of course, that the best interest of constituents may be expected to merge often with the best interests of the entire polity)?

By way of summary, what do these theories tell us about who is the "best" representative? If you were the representative, would you take a stand and let history be the judge? Or would you simply see what your constituents wanted, act accordingly, and argue that continuation in office at least guarantees continued influence? Does courage merely look good in the history books while failing to address life's immediate problem—personal survival and the necessity of compromise? Which choice would make you the "best" representative?

Before you try to decide how you would wish to behave if you were a representative (that is to say, what model of behavior would you wish to follow), you may find it useful to consider two classic studies of legislators and their relationship to constituencies. In 1959, Eulau, Wahlke, Buchanan and Ferguson[1] studied legislators in four states (New Jersey, Ohio, Tennessee, and California) by taking the polar extremes of trustee and instructed delegate and adding to them the in-between concept, "politico." The concept of politico recognizes that a representative's voting may move now toward the trustee end of the scale, then toward the instructed delegate end of the scale, depending on the type of issue to be decided. The politico, in short, adjusts his or her behavior according to the type of issue, recognizing that certain issues permit more independence and latitude of action than do others.

The second classic study touching on these matters was reported by Miller and Stokes in 1963. Their work, which compared the attitudes and issue preferences of a sample of members of Congress to the attitudes and issue preferences of their constituents regarding several different policy topics or domains, added a third model, the "responsible party government" model, to the trustee model and the instructed delegate model described above. Whereas the politico model is based on the relationship between a representative and his or her district, the responsible party government model is based on the relationship of a representative to citizens living outside, as well as inside, the constituency but supporting the same party to which the representative belongs. As Miller and Stokes put it, "Candidates of [national] legislative office appeal to the electorate in terms of a *national* party program and leadership, to which, if elected, they will be committed. Expressions of policy preference by the local district retains only the arithmetical significance that whichever party can rally to its program the greater number of supporters in the district will control its legislative seat."[2]

Just as the Eulau et al. study had suggested different models for different issue domains, so too Miller and Stokes found a correspondence between a given model and a certain type of issue. It will be useful for you to stop at this point and consider, what type of issue do you think is likely to go with which model? That is to say, which types of issues are likely to evoke which types of behavior by representatives?

We'll give you a clue. Think of three policy domains—social welfare legislation, civil rights legislation, and foreign policy enactments. Which domain do you think should be associated with which model? (Your instructor may wish to explore this topic during the debriefing of the simulation.)

The Simulation

Stage One: The Issues

The Subcommittee on Revision of the Constitution of the Judiciary Committee of the Lower House of the Atlantis National Assembly has before it for consideration today two proposed amendments to the Atlantis Constitution. Texts of the amendments will be provided by your instructor as needed. As will be noted in the following discussion of the "Simulation Run," the first stage of the simulation will involve four of the subcommittee members in discussion with their constituents. The Alpha constituents will be discussing one of the proposed amendments, and the Beta constituents a different one.

Stage Two: Running the Simulation ───────────

NOTE: A brief explanation of the principles of Parliamentary Procedure is located in the Appendix. You will find especially useful for reference during the simulation run the Rank Order of Commonly Used Motions (p. 219) and the Sequence of Motions chart (p. 219).

The Roles

The Members of the Subcommittee

1. The Legislator from the Province of Alpha

2. The Legislator from the Province of Beta

3. The Legislator from the Province of Delta

4. The Legislator from the Province of Omega

The Chair of the Subcommittee

5. The Legislator from the Province of Gamma

The chair of the subcommittee is free, as are the other legislators, to play himself or herself. Each must decide whether to act as a trustee or as an instructed delegate.

In a small group such as this subcommittee problems of parliamentary procedure are highly unlikely. In a pinch the assistance of the instructor as parliamentarian can be sought.

The class will be divided into groups of citizens from four provinces.

Sequence of Events

The first day of the simulation will be divided into two segments.

In the first segment, the members meet with their constituents; in the second segment, the members meet as a legislative committee.

Meetings with Constituents

At the beginning of the class period, five individuals will be identified as the Legislators from the Provinces of Alpha, Beta, Gamma, Delta, and Omega. The Legislator from Gamma will be named as subcommittee chair.

The remainder of the class will be divided into four groups. There will be no constituents from Gamma.

Legislators from Alpha and Beta: Each of you will be given a proposed amendment to the Atlantis Constitution (two different amendments), and you are to consult with your constituents to probe their opinions and values concerning the topic of the amendment. *At no time should you take a poll or ask for a show of hands.* Your task is to get an understanding of how your constituents feel about the issue and why. About five or six minutes will be allowed for this.

Probably the best way to begin is to say to the group, after you have seated yourselves in a conversation circle, "Here is a proposed amendment to the Atlantis Constitution. I'd like to hear your thoughts, as citizens of (Alpha or Beta), about the desirability of this amendment. What is your reaction to it?" Then read the amendment aloud, listen to their comments, and ask questions if you wish. *Remember: do not take a poll or a straw vote.* Also keep in mind the time constraint.

At the close of the discussion you will attend a meeting of the Subcommittee of the Lower House of the National Assembly, where several proposed constitutional amendments will be introduced.

Be sure to read the section entitled, "The Legislator from Gamma" p. 85 for details on what happens next.

Legislators from Delta and Omega: Each of you will discuss a proposed constitutional amendment with your respective constituents. *No decision will be made at this time* on this proposed amendment. This issue will be dealt with later in the semester. (NOTE: Your instructor will inform you if you are to use the issue which follows or if a different issue is to be discussed.)

The purpose of the discussion by the Delta and Omega constituents is twofold. First, it is useful for the legislator and constituents to get to know each other; second, it will be very helpful for the legislator to sense whether his/her constituents seem to have tendencies toward liberal or conservative views. About five or six minutes will be allowed for this.

The Constitution of Atlantis now states, "The National Assembly shall pass no law abridging the freedom of religion."

The activities of the Nature People (see pp. 6 and 173) have been a source of intense controversy wherever they engage in their rather unusual religious practices. Recently the province of Alpha passed a law restricting the activities of the Nature People. The law did not make any attempt to interfere with the beliefs of the Nature People, it merely restricted their right to engage in their activities in public. No attempt was made by the legislation to define such terms as "activities" or "public."

The Atlantis Constitution does not apply to the controversy, for its section on religion states, "The National Assembly shall pass no law abridging the freedom of religion."

An amendment has been suggested to extend the protection of religious freedom to the provincial level by amending the above language as follows:

"Neither a provincial legislature nor the National Assembly shall pass any law abridging the freedom of religion."

When the Delta citizens and the Omega citizens have seated themselves in respective discussion circles the representative may begin by saying,

"Here is a proposed amendment to the Atlantis Constitution. I'd like to hear your thoughts, as citizens of (Delta or Omega), about the desirability of this amendment. How do you feel about the right of a province to regulate behavior which is claimed to be religious? Should any behavior be permitted, regardless of how outrageous, or perhaps even harmful, it may seem to others?"

Be sure to read the proposed amendment aloud, listen to their comments, and ask questions if you wish. Since this amendment will not be discussed at this simulation session, there is no need to take a poll or straw vote. Keep in mind the time constraint.

Meeting of the Legislative Committee

At the close of the discussion you will attend a meeting of the Subcommittee of the Lower House of the National Assembly, where several proposed constitutional amendments will be introduced.

Be sure to read the section entitled, "The Legislator from Gamma" for details on what happens next.

The Legislator from Gamma: Your role in this simulation will be to serve as chair (presiding officer) of the Subcommittee on Constitutional Revision. The committee has before it two proposed amendments to the Atlantis Constitution, and your committee should consider and come to a decision on each.

Each amendment may be reworded or altered as the majority of the committee thinks best, and each amendment should be disposed of (perhaps after itself being amended) by being approved or disapproved through formal vote of the committee.

As presiding officer you may not introduce or second a motion, but you are entitled to vote on all matters coming to a vote within the committee. Also, you are entitled to comment, although your comments are likely to be conditioned by your awareness of your responsibility to promote a decision on each issue.

Your instructor will give you the language of each amendment that you are to consider. While the other committee members are talking with their constituents, you probably will want to review the summary of parliamentary procedure in the Appendix. Remember that the discussion can be relatively informal so long as there is not an objection or disagreement. The purpose of parliamentary procedure is to facilitate orderly progress toward a decision and to maintain civility in circumstances having a potential for discord and hostility. So, "stay loose." (If you are in doubt, feel free to refer to the parliamentarian, your instructor.) The probabilities are that your chief responsibility will not involve formal procedure questions; rather, it will be to keep the discussion moving toward a decision on each amendment within the time constraints.

Seating arrangements of the subcommittee will be as follows:

Alpha	Beta	Gamma	Delta	Omega

The subcommittee chair will permit a maximum of 15 minutes for discussion, amendment, and vote on each proposed amendment. The subcommittee may revise the wording if it wishes. *No member of the class will be allowed to participate in the discussion or voting.*

Each member of the class will be asked to answer the questions which appear on the Issue Preference Questionnaire. That page should be handed in to the instructor before leaving the classroom.

Stage Three: Debriefing and Critique ————

Your instructor will inform you when this will begin.

NOTE: Your instructor may ask you to complete and turn in the evaluation form which will be found on the page following the questionnaire.

1. Heinz Eulau, et al., ''The Role of the Representative: Some Empirical Observations on the Theory of Edmund Burke,'' *American Political Science Review,* 53 (September 1959): 742–756.
2. Warren E. Miller and Donald E. Stokes, ''Constituency Influence in Congress,'' in *Political Behavior in America,* Heinz Eulau, ed. (New York: Random House, 1966) p. 366. Reprinted from *American Political Science Review,* 57 (March 1963): 45–56.

Issue Preference Questionnaire

Please answer the following questions *at the end of the first day of the simulation and hand it to your instructor before leaving class.*

1. Of what province are you a citizen?

    _____ Alpha

    _____ Beta

    _____ Delta

    _____ Omega

2. If a referendum election were held now, how would you vote on the amendment discussed by the citizenry of Alpha?

    _____ for the amendment

    _____ against the amendment

3. If a referendum election were held now, how would you vote on the amendment discussed by the citizenry of Beta?

    _____ for the amendment

    _____ against the amendment

4. If an election were to be held tomorrow, what would be your reaction to the five legislators? (They are listed in the same order as they were seated, left to right.)

	Alpha	Beta	Gamma	Delta	Omega
Strongly support					
Somewhat support					
No opinion (neutral)					
Somewhat oppose					
Strongly oppose					

Evaluation Form **Simulation Four**

1. In comparison with other courses, or portions of courses, which you have taken, how would you rate this simulation experience?

2. What do you consider to be the most important thing (or things) you learned from the simulation?

3. Was there anything about the simulation which you found disappointing?

4. Do you have any suggestions as to how the simulation might be improved?

5. Suppose a friend had a choice of introductory American Government sections, one of which used simulations such as the one you just experienced. The friend asks you whether he or she should choose the section offering the simulation. What would your advice be?

Please indicate whether your role was:
    _____ Legislator
    _____ Constituent

If more space is needed, the opposite side of this page may be used. If you wish to suggest changes or improvements in the simulation, please do so. Thank you.

The Dilemmas of Executive Budget Making

Bureaucratic Goals, Limited Resources, and Public Demands

*When Congress finally gave up
primary responsibility for preparing
the budget in 1921, . . . abdicating an
ancient function it could no longer
perform, it gave a tremendous boost
to the power of the President, not
only to control his administration,
but to influence the legislative
process.*

Clinton Rossiter
The American Presidency

Introduction

Today in the United States the process of budget making is viewed as an "executive branch" type of function, but it was not always thus. Early budget making was in the hands of legislative assemblies, for only they had the power to appropriate money. Later, as governments increased the number and the scope of their activities, budget making became more and more a responsibility of the executive branch. The reasons for the shift of responsibility for the budget were several. First, the operations of administrative departments and bureaus produced a first-hand awareness of problems, of needs for responses to the problems, and of existing programs and policies. Second, the expertise to design useful responses to these problems very often was to be found within the bureaus of the executive branch. Third, the pyramidal (hierarchical) structure of the executive branch permitted hard decisions and reconciliation of conflicting views to be funnelled to one location, the desk of the chief executive. Thus it was that Congress, in 1921, transferred the task of making the budget to the president—one of the most significant shifts in the balance of power in the history of the republic.

Of course a chief executive has many advisers, including a budget director if the governmental unit is a large city, a state, or the national government, and in practice many budget decisions are made by persons other than the chief executive. But in principle the chief executive is responsible, rather like the way in which a military commander is responsible for actions of subordinates.

Simulations of this executive-type budget making, which is ultimately and essentially decision making by a single individual, are much less informative than simulations of decision making by a group, be it large or small. Group decision making reveals better the competition among different interests and factions for the always limited resources. For that reason, and in order to illustrate certain difficulties and tendencies, in this simulation a small group is employed as the decision maker. Imagine, if you wish, that the chief executive has a Budget Committee, whose role is advisory to the chief executive. Or, if you prefer, say to yourself that this group has no exact counterpart, but it nevertheless will reproduce concerns and considerations which have real world counterparts exceeding one's capacity to count. Whichever way you prefer to look at this committee's role, the experience should reveal to you some of the difficulties which arise when one tries to grapple with the problem of dividing up a sum of money.

One often has the feeling from American radio, television, newspapers, and magazines that the struggle for appropriations is between the contending forces of the heartless versus the treasonous. The arguments seem to be based on the assumption that the trade-offs are between the suffering poor and essential defense programs. Thus, if only an "unneeded" and probably all-too-soon-obsolete weapons system could be cut from the budget, there would be money enough for all the needy. The converse argument proposes that all the alleged needy aren't really suffering that much and what should be done is to cut such programs to the bone, protecting those truly in need, while beefing up our defenses so as to protect our country. It is easy to forget that there is much hyperbole ("hype" in advertising jargon) in all this argument. Every bureaucratic agency sees its role as having an importance factor ranging from essential to vital for national survival. This is true of city, state or federal agencies—even university agencies. The job of each agency chief is to argue persuasively and to struggle as aggressively as possible to help the agency do a better job. Thus the army will always need more and better weapons, more soldiers, and better pay in order to retain high quality personnel. The air force needs better, faster, more advanced planes, more rockets; the navy more ships, and so on. Likewise, agencies concerned for the needy will always want to reach out to help more of those in need and constantly will identify more groups in need.

Yet the struggle is not merely between compassion and defense. Less altruistic factors are also at work. Aid for the needy involves benefits for nursing homes, social workers, doctors, nurses, hospitals, the drug industry, and so on. Aid for defense means large sums for aircraft manufacturers, labor unions, plus all those support industries which prosper when workers have money to spend. The local tavern and the local independent grocery also have a stake in ensuring the continued prosperity of the local defense plant, shipyards, army base, hospital, or any other source of local income.

We must not forget that behind the very real ideological conflict of defense versus human needs is the equally important struggle between those who benefit and those who pay. At the level of state politics, for example, where defense needs are not an issue, the conflicts over budget allocations are just as intense. College students attending publicly supported universities (and university faculty, staff and administrators) are engaging in an identical activity when they ask for more aid for higher education. At whose expense? Since most states cannot go into debt, the state leaders must make hard choices: raise taxes or give program A more than program B. Who benefits? Who loses? If colleges get more subsidy, enabling students to attend for less tuition money, then that lowered cost to students is being paid by someone else. Who should pay the added cost?

For this simulation, the problem has been simplified, but it is not simple. You will not have to choose between national defense and human needs nor wrestle with the problem of who pays. As with city and state political leaders, your task will be to make choices from among the competing demands of various human needs and services.

As you approach this simulation it may be useful to bear in mind a few questions. First, is it difficult or is it easy for a legislative body to develop a priority system to guide its decisions on appropriation matters? What priorities are used by participants in the simulation? How are they derived or developed?

Second, what is the importance of incrementalism—of starting with the current year's appropriation and perhaps adding marginal amounts to reflect changing circumstances next year? An alternative approach to budgeting is called zero-based budgeting. Instead of taking this year's budget as given and then asking whether next year's budget should be increased, decreased, or held at the same level (i.e., incrementalism), zero-based budgeting starts with a clean slate. The wisdom of continuing the agency (or the program) is challenged, and justification for the continuation is an essential part of the budget-making process for next year's expenditures. Which approach characterizes the simulation?

Third, is it difficult or is it easy to enlarge one appropriation by reducing another? When resources are finite, do dollar amounts get moved around from one category to another with ease? It should be noted in this connection that U.S. federal budget making is more open-ended because of the ability of the federal government to borrow, to incur deficit financing. (But note that eventually the size of the federal deficit can become a concern, as it has since 1982, even though a president is not constrained as is the typical governor, who is forbidden by the state constitution to incur any deficit whatsoever.)

Fourth, is it difficult or is it easy to accommodate new functions and organizations? What happens when a worthy new objective or organization comes onto the budget-making scene? As you think about possible answers to these questions, and as you apply the questions to the activities of the simulation, it is our hope and expectation that you will come to a fuller understanding of budget making and its problems.

One point to keep in mind is the difficulty faced by the Budget Committee in evaluating programs. Note, for example, the problems one faces when comparing national parks with wildlife protection. Parks are relatively easy to evaluate. Usage can be quantified and justified. There is a faithful and reliable constituency—the users—who can create political pressure to maintain support for the parks. The value of wildlife protection, on the other hand, is very difficult to quantify. How does one know how much money to put into the project? How much wildlife should one seek to protect? What is the natural constituency for wildlife protection? Environmentalists support such programs, of course. But whereas park users represent a broad spectrum of the public and can be counted on as a reliable and continuous source of support, environmentalists find it more difficult to maintain their influence. Public support is often fickle, its ardor for preservation and conservation at times dampened by the claims of conflicting groups (developers, hunters, mining and logging interests) and conflicting objectives (energy needs, defense needs).

The Setting

Inflation in Atlantis has been running at about 15% each year. President Jaworski has pledged that inflation must be brought under control and, in order to do this, he is determined that the national government will limit spending to a 10% increase for next year. The task of sifting through all the requests for money and listening to the testimony of all departments has been delegated by the President to a Presidential Budget Committee. It has been an enormous task and has taken weeks, even though the committee has imposed severe time limits on each person testifying. At long last, the committee has arrived at this point in the process. All the departments have been heard, the committee has made almost all of its decisions and remained *overall* within the presidential mandate of a maximum total budget increase of 10%. Obviously, this does not mean everyone simply received a 10% increase; some gained more, some less.

Eight agencies remain. A brief description of the functions of each agency follows, including an indication of their appropriation for the current year, plus their request for next year. You will note that the Presidential Budget Committee has a problem: the total amount requested by the eight agencies exceeds the permitted 10% increase. While in a real situation, such a committee (or person) would be free to take money from anywhere in the budget to meet the requests of these last agencies to be considered, its assignment here is to view these eight as if they were the entire list. And, as you will discover, the problem of dealing with budget requests is the same if you have eight or a thousand. How does one decide who gets what? If one merely increases everyone by a fixed percentage, what does one do about new needs, new challenges? The Budget Committee has the agency budgets for this current year. You will note that the total for these eight agencies, plus 10% (the amount the President has stated as the maximum he will support when he sends next year's budget to the legislature for approval) is considerably less than the amount requested by these eight agencies. How will the Budget Committee meet this challenge?

The Simulation

Stage One: The Issue

Simulations Five and Six are intended to illustrate different stages and aspects of the process of budget making and appropriation. Your instructor may wish to use both of them or perhaps only one. A brief explanation of each follows:

1. Simulation Five. As is described in the introductory portion of this topic, the first stage of the budget process involves an executive branch function. The chief executive (or his or her staff) has to decide how estimated revenue will be divided up among the functions of many agencies whose tasks are quite different. In our simulation, this assignment has been given to a Budget Committee, which must approve, modify, or reject funding requests of programs which range from abortion clinics, to wildlife protection, to marine safety, to senior citizen centers—just to name a few. It is important to remember that this is a committee of the Executive Branch.

    You should also remember that the Budget Committee will be recommending to the chief executive what each agency should get next year. Our simulation assumes that the President will accept the recommendations of the Budget Committee.

2. Simulation Six. After it has been approved by the Budget Committee (i.e., the President), the budget proposal is then sent to the National Assembly where the Appropriations Committee will consider (read "review, revise, revile, and finally ratify") the budget.

Stage Two: *Preparing for the Simulation*————

You will be assigned a role by your instructor. If you are assigned to the Budget Committee you will be part of a relatively small group having responsibility for making the final decisions on the requests sent forward from the various agencies. If you are assigned an agency role it will be an agency whose budget recommendation has not yet been settled by the Budget Committee. There may well be several participants assigned to each agency, and you must consult with your fellow agency representatives as to the strategy you will follow in responding to questions from the Budget Committee members. An agency delegation may wish to identify one of its members to speak on behalf of the agency, but each agency may handle the possibility of questions as it sees fit.

In any event, individual agency members should not feel constrained from speaking.

Following receipt of your role assignment you should, if you are assigned a role as an agency representative, do two things. First, you should identify the other members of the class who have been assigned roles in your agency, and you should arrange to confer with them on the matters mentioned above. Second, you should familiarize yourself thoroughly with the information concerning your agency, its programs, its budget needs, and its place among the competing needs of government which have yet to be decided by the Budget Committee.

Roles 1–10: Representatives of the Abortion Clinics Program

The issue in Atlantis is not the permissibility of abortion. That has come to be accepted as a matter of personal conscience, and a majority of the people support this view. What remains controversial is the issue of public funding of abortion, which in effect exacts support both from those who approve abortion and from those who oppose it on moral grounds.

Current practice fully funds abortion on demand for any woman whose family income is below the minimum maintenance level. This may appear as a fairly straightforward issue, but there are two complicating factors. The first of these is the difference in the percentage of those in the poverty category: Alpha, Beta, Gamma, Delta—8.6%; Omega—20%.

The second factor is the difference in the cultural attitudes toward abortion. Omegans are very conservative, and only one percent (1%) of the women who are in households below the median income and who are of childbearing age (16–40) have an abortion in a given year. Alpha and Gamma are somewhat less conservative than Omega, and two percent (2%) of the women below median income and of childbearing age seek abortions in any one year. The least conservative province, as one might expect, is Beta. Perhaps surprising to some, Delta, while it is culturally quite unlike Beta, has a similarly high rate of abortion seeking— ten percent (10%) for women of childbearing age from households below the median income.

Here are some facts the Budget Committee will need in order to make its recommendations:

1. The cost of an abortion is A$50. (''A$'' = Atlantis dollars.) (The 15% inflation rate will increase this to A$57.50 next year.)

2. Public funding for abortions this year totaled A$3,303,250. This amount covered the cost of abortions for all women in the poverty category who sought them, and it takes into account the differential rates of abortion-seeking within the poverty category among the provinces.

3. The Abortion Clinics Program leadership has proposed that for next year the staff of the clinics be enlarged so that all women in the minimum maintenance income category will be able to have abortions fully paid for out of public funds. This will require an additional A$7,112,060 (adjusted for 15% inflation). The figure takes into account the differential rates of minimum maintenance levels and abortion in the provinces.

Table 3: Budget Proposal for the Abortion Clinics Program

(A$ = Atlantis Dollars)

	Appropriated for Current Year	Agency Recommended Budget for Next Year
Abortion requested by women in poverty income level. Full funding. (66,065)†	A$3,303,250	A$3,798,738*
Abortions requested by women in minimum maintenance income level. Full funding. (123,688)†	— 0 —	7,112,060*
Total subsidy for abortion clinics	A$3,303,250	A$10,910,798
Increase permitted for next year by the administration (10%)‡	330,325	
Total authorized continuation budget	A$3,633,575	A$3,633,575
Shortage		A$7,277,223

*Adjusted for 15% inflation.
†Takes into account differential abortion rates in the provinces.
‡The administration projects a 10% growth in tax revenues for next year and has instructed each agency to prepare a ''continuation budget'' which is limited to current expenditures plus 10%.

Roles 11–20: Representatives of the Crisis Centers Program

Some years ago, the national government began funding crisis centers. Identification of the need for such centers grew out of the women's movement, a factor in the politics of Atlantis as it was in the United States. The program was very modest in its early years, consisting primarily of just a few centers located in the largest cities. The usefulness of these initial efforts in assisting female victims of assault and rape led to demands for the establishment of centers throughout Atlantis.

The activities of the center are mostly those of a counseling and advising nature. Thus the centers have no medical facilities but serve rather as a referral agency to make sure the victims of rape are admitted to a hospital familiar with the evidentiary aspects of the problem and that the police are alerted that a crime has been committed. Rape victims often do not know where to go or what to do in order to receive both proper medical assistance and to assist the police and the prosecutor in gathering evidence against an accused rapist. Thus the centers have developed cooperative procedures so that the victim is cared for, the needed photographic and medical evidence is collected immediately, and the police are assisted (and prodded, when necessary) in their efforts to find the rapist. Other activities include psychological counseling for women victims of domestic violence, especially when it was inflicted by a relative or spouse. Referrals in this case involve the identification of appropriate relief agencies to find housing, perhaps medical care if needed, and/or sources of assistance in cases where the victim is trying to deal with such problems as the trauma of suddenly being alone, without funds, without skills, perhaps even with suicidal tendencies, and perhaps with young children.

Crisis centers are now located throughout Atlantis, but the number of such centers varies considerably from province to province. The primary reason for this is not political, but the financial realities caused by variations in population density. Where population is concentrated in a number of large cities, as it is on Alpha and Beta, it is much simpler to reach the affected individuals, for very few women live far from a crisis center. But where there are many small towns scattered throughout the countryside, as on Gamma, Delta, and Omega, the problem becomes quite difficult to solve. To establish a center in every little town would be a prohibitively expensive undertaking; to establish them only in major cities would mean that some women would never be able to get to a center. An unhappy, but perhaps realistic, compromise was reached, and what is called the "model center" ratio was established. This "model center" should not be viewed as an ideal, but rather as an adequate minimum. Here are the facts the Budget Committee will need to know:

1. A "model center" is used as a funding model. The concept is used to describe the resources and the costs of a center which would serve a typical city of 100,000 persons. The costs incorporated by the model then become the basis for calculating the national government's contribution to the provincial government for support of a crisis center. The provincial government is free, if it chooses, to add funds to broaden the scope of service, to establish more centers, etc. But the Atlantis contribution is determined by a combination of the model cost and the ratio of centers to population in that province, which enables one to calculate how many "model centers" the province is entitled to receive from the Atlantis government. (See #4 below.) A "model center" has a staff of two professionals and one clerk-secretary-receptionist.

2. The cost of this "model center" is A$9,000 ("A$" = Atlantis dollars) per year (personnel—A$6,000; office operations— A$3,000). Adjusted for 15% inflation, this figure will be A$10,350.

3. This "model center" staff has been found to be adequate to meet the demands for assistance of women who are victims of rape or domestic violence.

4. The population ratios that have been used to determine how many "centers" (i.e., how many center equivalents) each province is entitled to, how many staff they will be authorized, are as follows:

	Ratio of centers to population
Alpha and Beta—70% urbanized NOTE: This means that the goal is to have no more than 5% of the population beyond 80 kilometers (50 miles) range of some center; that is, 95% of the population is within 80 kilometers (50 miles) of a center.	1/100,000
Gamma and Delta—50% urbanized NOTE: This means that the goal is to have no more than 15% of the population beyond 100 kilometers (62 miles) range of some center; that is, 85% of the population is within 100 kilometers (62 miles) of a center.	1/300,000
Omega—30% urbanized NOTE: No distance criterion has been established.	1/500,000

5. The estimate is that a "model center" should be able to deal with about 700 cases per year of women in need of counseling, referral, and follow up because of rape or domestic violence.

   Now, however, the crisis centers are facing several types of criticism. Too many women are simply unable to receive assistance in the provinces where low population density has brought about the use of larger ratios, resulting in fewer centers, both absolutely

Table 4: Comparison of Number of Crisis Centers Produced by Using Existing Ratios versus the Proposed Ratios

	Existing Ratios Number of "Model Centers"*	Proposed Ratios Number of "Model Centers"
Alpha	213 (1/100,000)	213 (1/100,000)
Beta	211 (1/100,000)	211 (1/100,000)
Gamma	60 (1/300,000)	87 (1/200,000)
Delta	51 (1/300,000)	76 (1/200,000)
Omega	21 (1/500,000)	53 (1/200,000)
Total Number of Centers	556	640

*The "model center" concept is a way of planning costs, not necessarily an actual center. Thus Alpha's 213 "centers" mean it is authorized the equivalent of 213 × A$9,000, or A$1,917,000. Actual location of the centers, determination of the number of such centers in the province, and the staff size in a particular center are administrative matters.

Table 5: Budget Proposal for the Crisis Centers Program

(A$ = Atlantis Dollars)

	Appropriated for the Current Year	Agency Recommended Budget for Next Year
"Model Centers" now established (556) (at A$9,000 each)	A$5,004,000	A$5,754,600*
Increase of 84 "model centers" to eliminate some of the differential caused by differences in provincial population density. Gamma, Delta, and Omega would then be funded according to ratio of one center per 200,000 population (at A$10,350 each)	— 0 —	869,400*
Addition of equivalent of 1/2 full-time child psychologist in each "model center" to meet needs of child victims. (A$1250 × 640)	— 0 —	800,000
Addition of equivalent of 1/4 full-time male case worker in each "model center" to meet the needs of male victims. (A$625 × 640)	— 0 —	400,000
Total support Crisis Centers	A$5,004,000	A$7,824,000
Increase permitted for next year by the administration (10%)†	500,400	
Total authorized continuation budget	A$5,504,400	A$5,504,400
Shortage		A$2,319,600

*Adjusted for 15% inflation.
†The administration projects a 10% growth in the revenues for next year and has instructed each agency to prepare a "continuation budget" which is limited to current expenditures plus 10%.

and relatively. In addition, many women must travel quite far in order to receive such assistance as is available.

Minimal assistance is currently available for child victims of sexual assault or physical violence. Only recently have centers been trying to help child victims, and this has created work loads for the staff far beyond what they have either the time or the expertise to handle. It is quite apparent, for example, that each "model center" should include the expertise of a child psychologist in addition to the two professionals in each "center."

No provision has ever been made to address the problem of male victims. While not numerous, male victims of domestic violence are nevertheless appearing in increasing numbers at the centers. The assailant may be the spouse, an adult child, or a relative. In one case, a severely beaten man had been victimized by his wife and daughter. Since the centers have neither mandate nor staff to handle such cases, all are turned away and merely urged to report the assault to the police.

As you will note, the proposed budget for next year proposes several increases to meet the cost of these new services.

Roles 21–30: Representatives of the Day-Care Centers Program

Atlantis has experienced a phenomenon familiar to Americans: large numbers of pre-school children have both parents working or a single parent who works. The demand for and use of day-care centers has grown very rapidly. Yet the cost of this service is not cheap. Here are some facts the Budget Committee must consider:

1. Annual cost of operations of a typical day-care center, serving a maximum of 23 children:

One professional	A$1,200
Two aides at A$600	1,200
Supplies, rent, utilities, etc.	1,000
Total annual cost of operations of a typical center	A$3,400
(A$ = Atlantis dollars)	

2. For the past four years the Atlantis government has been funding either some portion or all of the cost of day-care centers for children of needy families. Families pay different amounts for day-care for a child, depending on family income. The actual cost per child for 12 months of day care averages out to A$150. Thus this is the amount supplied for children whose family income is at the poverty income level. Half that amount (A$75) on average is provided to children whose family income is at the minimum maintenance level; one-quarter of that amount (A$37.50) is provided for those whose family income is below

the median income level. (Adjusted for inflation, these figures will be A$172.50; A$86.25; and A$43.13.)

3. As you would expect, not all mothers or fathers with eligible children will use day-care centers. Unemployable parents will have no need for a day-care center. Some parents will be concerned for the safety of their children or about the quality of the care and nurture at the center. Some parents will prefer to leave their children with grandparents or other relatives. Because of the inconvenience of travel to the center, some parents will find it easier to keep the children at home.

Table 6: Budget Proposal for the Day-Care Centers Program

(A$ = Atlantis Dollars)

	Appropriated for the Current Year	Agency Recommended Budget for Next Year
Full funding of poverty level	A$55,102,800	A$63,368,220*
Half funding of minimum maintenance level	33,061,650	38,020,897*
Quarter funding of those with income below the median	8,265,412	9,505,224*
Total cost of program	A$96,429,862	A$110,894,341*
Increase permitted for next year by the administration (10%)†	9,642,986	
Total authorized continuation budget	A$106,072,848	A$106,072,848
Shortage		A$4,821,493

*Adjusted for 15% inflation.
†The administration projects a 10% growth in tax revenues for next year and has instructed each agency to prepare a "continuation budget" which is limited to current expenditures plus 10%.

4. For the purposes of this simulation, it is assumed that, proportionate to population, there is uniform distribution throughout the provinces of children in need of day-care services.

5. The following table shows the number of children attending government day-care centers, according to subsidy levels.

Income Level	Number of Children
Full funding (Poverty Level Income)	367,352
Half funding (Minimum Maintenance Income Level)	440,822
Quarter funding (Income Below Median)	220,411

Roles 31–40: Representatives of the Marine Safety and Rescue Service

One of the earliest traditions on the islands which came to be known as Atlantis was the Marine Safety and Rescue Service. The rescue service dates back to the time before the provinces were officially established by the United Nations and when population was thinly settled along the coastlines. Not surprisingly, shipping was an important activity, and it became a matter of great pride for the citizens of the small coastal towns to volunteer to take part in the rescue of passengers and crews of ships in distress. Numerous potential victims of storms were saved by the brave volunteer rescue crews, and many local heroes found their niche in local history. Local legends are replete with the tales of vicious storms, great courage and tragic deaths.

The local volunteer crews and the marine stations which sponsor them still perform important services. Classes are held on the development of basic skills of seamanship, there are free schools on watercraft safety and navigation, and all this is done by the volunteers. Marine Rescue Days, as they are called, continue to be held as an annual celebration, and the rescue boats compete to bring honor to their towns, to break records, and to immortalize the crews. As a result of all these activities, the Marine Safety and Rescue Service continues to have a strong political base. The local towns view Marine Rescue Days as vital to the maintenance of strong community feelings, a means of preserving an honored history while simultaneously uniting newcomers with the towns' historic residents. It is provincialism in its best sense, meaning local identity, local pride. Consequently, the towns collectively request support for the Marine Safety and Rescue Service. The total financial support is modest, but it is essential to the continuation of the service, for it pays for the equipment (the boats, the marine radio transmitter and receiver, the storage sheds), the year-round staff (to monitor weather reports and relay distress messages or reports, to maintain the equipment), and of course the expenses related to the celebration (prizes, subsidy for the annual clambake, etc.).

Fifty towns scattered throughout the five provinces maintain these rescue services. Volunteers still meet weekly to keep the boats and the crews in shape; the marine radio, though quite antiquated, continues to transmit and receive; each town still holds its annual week-long celebration. In order to perpetuate the traditions, the local volunteer crews still struggle to save the "victims of the sea," but while the storms are as frequent as ever, the crises are not, and rarely is there a victim in danger. In reality, the Marine Safety and Rescue Service is an anachronism. The actual rescuing is handled now by heavily powered and radar/sonar-guided launches and helicopters operating from regionally located bases. The Marine Safety and Rescue Service, given its

Table 7: Budget Proposal for Marine Safety Rescue Service

(A$ = Atlantis Dollars)

	Appropriated for the Current Year	Agency Recommended Budget for Next Year
Equipment maintenance†	A$ 15,000	A$ 17,250*
Marine radio repair†	37,500	43,125*
Personnel (year-round, 24-hour service to monitor and relay messages on marine radio)†	175,000	201,250*
Marine Rescue Day Celebration†	15,000	17,250*
Total support for Marine Safety Rescue Service	A$242,500	A$278,875*
Increase permitted for next year by the administration (10%)‡	24,250	
Total authorized continuation budget	A$266,750	A$266,750
Shortage		A$ 12,125

*Adjusted for 15% inflation.
†Total based on cost for 50 towns.
‡The administration projects a 10% growth in tax revenues for next year and has instructed each agency to prepare a "continuation budget" which is limited to current expenditures plus 10%.

long traditions, resisted the establishment of modernized, but regionally located, rescue services. Thus it was that the Atlantis Navy assumed the tasks of rescuing crews and passengers and the MSRS gradually accepted the new world in which they merely celebrated the rescues of the past. As for the MSRS, it preserved its name, its traditions, and its activities, and it gave up its rescue function. But it still has a significant and strong political base.

The budget breakdown for a model town rescue service is as follows:

Rescue equipment maintenance (varnish for boats, repair of boats)	A$300
Marine radio repairs	750
Personnel (year-round, 24-hour service to monitor and relay messages on marine radio) (168 hours per week x 52 weeks = 8,736 x A$.40 per hour = A$3,500)	3,500
Marine Rescue Days Celebration	300
Total	A$4,850

Roles 41–50: Representatives of the National Parks Service

The National Parks Service currently administers four national parks, one each in Alpha, Beta, Gamma, and Delta. These four parks are all about the same size, with similar scales of operations. At present there is no national park in Omega; however, the budget for next year recommends that one be established.

The objectives of the park system are to administer the properties for the enjoyment and education of all the citizens of Atlantis and to protect the natural environment of the areas. The service develops and implements park management plans and staffs the areas under its administration. It relates the natural values and historical significance of each of the parks to the public through talks, tours, films, exhibits, and publications. It operates campgrounds and other visitor facilities and provides—usually through concessions—lodging, food, and transportation services.

The Budget for the National Parks Service consists of two major categories:

1. Parks Operation, which received a total of A$11 million for the current year. Since the park system generated A$2,000,000 in user fees, the net cost to the taxpayers was A$9,000,000. ("A$" = Atlantis dollars)

2. Park Development, which received A$4.5 million for the current year. This is the fourth year of a five-year acquisition plan to purchase land and then develop a new park in the desert-coastal area of Omega. (The first year of project development cost occurs next fiscal year, which also will be the last year of land acquisition costs.)

Table 8: Budget Proposal for the National Parks Service

(A$ = Atlantis Dollars)

	Appropriated for the Current Year	Agency Recommended Budget for Next Year
Parks Operations		
Education (naturalist programs, visitors' center)	A$ 1,200,000	A$ 1,380,000*
Safety (patrolling highways, response to medical emergencies, patrolling paths in response to complaints)	1,000,000	1,150,000*
Recreation (trail path maintenance, swimming pool, golf greens, tennis courts)	1,500,000	1,725,000*
Maintenance and service (janitorial, road repair, trash collection, water supply, sewage disposal)	7,300,000	8,395,000*
	A$11,000,000	A$12,650,000*
Income from user fees (general admission, camping, golf, tennis)†	2,000,000	2,000,000
Total net cost of operations	A$ 9,000,000	A$10,650,000
(See § note at end.)		
Park Development—Omega National Park		
Land acquisition	A$ 4,500,000	A$ 4,500,000
Development (this amount, plus inflation, will have to be expended for each of the next succeeding five years.)		

	Appropriated for the Current Year	Agency Recommended Budget for Next Year
Public recreation facilities		A$ 4,000,000
Water supply (deep wells, desalinization, water storage tank)		A$ 6,000,000
Harbor development		A$ 5,000,000
Roads and trails development		A$ 6,500,000
Airport		A$ 2,000,000
Sanitary sewers, sewage disposal plant		A$ 4,000,000
Total cost of park development	A$ 4,500,000	A$32,000,000
Total cost of operations and development	13,500,000	42,650,000
Total increase permitted for next year by the administration (10%)‡	1,350,000	
Total authorized continuation budget	A$14,850,000	A$14,850,000
Shortage		A$27,800,000

*Adjusted for 15% inflation.

†User fees may be increased. The total fee was raised last year from A$.60 to A$.80. However, it was discovered that as fees went up, park attendance declined. This fact was verified by a survey of park visitors. The following formula should be used to estimate amount of income from increased user fees.

Per Capita Amount of Fee	Number of Visitors Per Year	User Fee Revenue For Year
A$ .60	2,850,000	A$1,710,000
.80	2,500,000	2,000,000
1.00	2,250,000	2,250,000
1.20	2,000,000	2,400,000
1.40	1,700,000	2,380,000

‡The administration projects a 10% growth in tax revenues for next year and has instructed each agency to prepare a "continuation budget" which is limited to current expenditures plus 10%.

§NOTE: Parks operations expenses divide up as follows:

Personnel costs	55% of total
Transport (trucks, patrol cars, gas, oil, repairs)	18% of total
Supplies & Equipment (everything from toilet paper to blacktop to seedlings)	18% of total
Miscellaneous	9% of total
	100%

Support for the new park proposal comes from two sources. There is, as one can appreciate, an extremely strong demand for the park from Omegans. Provincial pride is clearly part of the explanation, but there is also the matter of a desire on the part of Omegans to have recreational and vacation facilities which are near enough to be enjoyed without great expense or travel time. Given the cold and damp climate of the settled areas of Omega, development of the coastal desert area, with its hot sun, would have a great attraction for the sun-starved Omegan citizens.

There is, however, one additional advantage in developing the coastal areas of the Omegan desert: the possibility of creating a tourist attraction which might tempt foreign visitors to come to Atlantis. Support for the new park, therefore, has more than a provincial base, for if foreign trade results it means the national balance of trade will be helped. It is easy to guess what will then happen. The private land proximate to the national park will begin to attract private developers—of hotels, condominiums, banks, vacation facilities, vacation homes, and on and on. The most visionary of the planners talk of a new Riviera. But none of this can occur without the start-up support.

Roles 51–60: Representatives of the Scholarships for College Students Program

The primary goal of the scholarship program has been to assist needy college students. Here are some facts the Budget Committee will need in order to understand how the program works and make its recommendations:

1. The population of Atlantis divides itself as follows in socioeconomic terms:

   - Poverty Level—family income below A$500 (A$ = Atlantis dollars)

   - Minimum Maintenance Level—family income between A$500–A$1,500)

   - Median Level—family income between A$1,500–A$3,500 (Actual median income is A$2,000)

   - Comfortable Level—family income between A$3,500–A$5,000

- Affluent Level—family income above A$5,000

2. Number and percent of high school graduates who went to college last year:

Income Level	No. of H.S. Graduates Last Year	Percent Who Went to College	No. Who Went to College
Poverty	102,102	1%	1,021
Minimum Maintenance	204,204	10	20,420
Up to the Median	204,204	25	51,051
Above the Median	204,204	25	51,051
Comfortable	204,204	60	122,522
Affluent	102,102	95	96,996
Total	1,021,020		343,061

3. College costs A$500 per academic year.

4. The policy adopted for the budget for the current fiscal year provided a national planning target of full funding (A$500) for all students whose families were in the poverty level, half funding (A$250) for all students whose families were in the minimum maintenance level, and one-quarter funding (A$125) for all students whose family incomes were below the median family income level. *But the actual distribution of money was by province on the basis of population, not on the basis of the number of needy in the population.* This legislative error was brought about because of haste in the passage of the appropriation bill.

   Stated another way, for each A$1,000 increment/decrement in the allocation next year, there will be a gain/loss of:

- 2 full scholarships (poverty level family income), or

- 4 half scholarships (minimum maintenance family income), or

- 8 quarter scholarships (up to the median family income).

5. The current year's budget allocation had some interesting omissions which the Department of Education has tried to ad-

dress in its budget proposals. No provision was made in earlier years for merit scholarships. All scholarship awards were based entirely on need. There has been extensive public criticism of this, especially by citizens whose incomes, while above the median, fall below the A$3,500 mark, which is identified as the minimum "comfortable" standard of living. Their argument stresses the unfairness of a system which places all of its emphasis on need and none on the scholarly achievements of students. They do not quarrel with helping those in need, only with the absence of incentives and support for academic achievers. In order to meet this demand, next year's budget proposal includes an item of A$57,500 for 100 full scholarships to be based on merit.

It has been a matter of concern to many citizens, and to those in charge of the scholarship program, that only 1% of the high school graduates whose family income falls in the poverty level go to college as compared with 95% of the affluent high school graduates. What is particularly regrettable about the low college attendance level of those in the poverty income group is that their standard test scores suggest that many more are qualified to go to college and might attend if more scholarships were available.

In an attempt to expand the opportunities for social mobility for talented young people who are not fortunate enough to have affluent parents, it has been recommended that an additional 1% of the high school graduates in the poverty level category be granted full scholarships. Next year's budget includes an item of A$587,075 to fund this objective of an additional 1,021 full scholarships.

Last year, 1,021 scholarships were authorized. The full scholarships were divided among the five provinces on the basis of population, as follows:

Province	Percentage of Population of Atlantis	Number of Scholarships When Distribution Is Based on Population %
Alpha	24.9%	254
Beta	24.7	252
Gamma	20.3	209
Delta	17.8	181
Omega	12.3	125
Total	100.0	1,021

Obviously, the larger and more prosperous provinces heartily approved of this arrangement. What is hidden in this allocation is the assumption that poverty is distributed approximately evenly throughout the five provinces; this tends to be correct—except for Omega. In fact, that 10% poverty factor divides up quite differently: in Alpha, Beta, Gamma, and Delta 8.6% of the families live below the poverty line, in Omega the figure is 20%!

As far as the Omegans are concerned, this is just one more example of blatant discrimination against them.

They are arguing—demanding—that the full scholarship allocation next year reflect the actual distribution of poverty, and be as follows:

High School Graduates	Province	Poverty Percentage	No. of Persons Below Poverty Level	No. of Poverty People Eligible to Go to College
254,234	Alpha	8.6%	21,864	219
252,192	Beta	8.6	21,689	217
207,267	Gamma	8.6	17,825	178
181,742	Delta	8.6	15,630	156
125,586	Omega	20.0	25,117	251
1,021,021			102,125	1,021

The impact of this is clear; four of the provinces are going to lose sizeable numbers of scholarships next year if Omega is given recognition for its unfortunate economic situation.

Province	No. of Scholarships Gained or (Lost)
Alpha	(35)
Beta	(35)
Gamma	(31)
Delta	(25)
Omega	126

There are several possible alternatives. One solution is to reallocate as suggested above, so that Omega's high poverty level is recognized. It seems very likely that the four original provinces will not accept this alternative gracefully. Since they are not very fond of Omega (or Omegans) anyhow, why should they make any sacrifices for them? Another solution is to continue the allocation system used this year, even though it discriminates against Omegans. Let the Omegans continue to accuse the other provinces of discrimination. A third solution is to increase the total number of full scholarships by 126, so that the four original provinces will not lose any scholarships, but the Omegan share will reflect its high level of poverty. The scholarship agency has opted for this alternative and included an item of A$72,450 in the budget proposed for next year to fund these additional 126 full scholarships.

Table 9: Budget Proposal for the College Scholarship Program

(A$ = Atlantis Dollars)

	Appropriated for the Current Year	Agency Recommended Budget for Next Year
Full scholarships (1,021)	A$ 510,500	A$ 587,075*
Full scholarships to fund additional 1% poverty level (1,021)	— 0 —	587,075
Full scholarships to be based on merit (100)	— 0 —	57,500
Full scholarships to assist Omega (126)	— 0 —	72,450
Half scholarships (20,420)	5,105,500	5,870,750*
Quarter scholarships (51,051)	6,381,375	7,338,581*
Total scholarship assistance for college students	A$11,996,875	A$14,513,431*
Increase permitted for next year by the administration (10%)†	1,199,687	
Total authorized continuation budget	A$13,196,562	A$13,196,562
Shortage		A$ 1,316,869

*Adjusted for 15% inflation. Full scholarship increased next year to A$575, half scholarship increased to A$287.50, quarter scholarship increased to A$143.75.
†The administration projects a 10% growth in tax revenues for next year and has instructed each agency to prepare a "continuation budget" which is limited to current expenditures plus 10%.

Roles 61–70: Representatives of the Senior Citizens Program

Only a decade or so ago, there were few government subsidized facilities in Atlantis for older people. The recreation rooms in churches were often scheduled for senior citizen activities on certain days, sometimes private social welfare agencies would sponsor such programs. Finally, responding to the political pressure of increasingly influential organizations, such as the AARP (Atlantis Association of Retired Persons), the Atlantis National Assembly passed a law which set as a goal the construction of a senior citizens center at a ratio of one center to each 50,000 population. It must be understood that the funding of the construction is based on the concept of a "model center," which for the current year costs A$50,000 ("A$" = Atlantis dollars). The concept is used to describe the resources and the costs of construction of a center which would serve a typical city of 50,000. The costs incorporated by the model then become the basis for calculating the national government's contribution to the provincial government, which decides on the location and the size of the actual centers.

Responsibility for the senior citizens center program has been divided up. The national government has undertaken the task of

Table 10: Budget Proposal for the Senior Citizens Centers Program

(A$ = Atlantis Dollars)

	Appropriated for the Current Year	Agency Recommended Budget for Next Year
Construction of Senior Citizens Centers—156 "model centers"† at A$50,000 each	A$7,800,000	A$8,970,000*
Increase permitted for next year by the administration (10%)‡	780,000	
Total authorized continuation budget	A$8,580,000	A$8,580,000
Shortage		A$ 390,000

*Adjusted for 15% inflation.
†The "model center" concept is a way of planning costs, not necessarily an actual center.
‡The administration projects a 10% growth in tax revenues for next year and has instructed each agency to prepare a "continuation budget" which is limited to current expenditures plus 10%.

construction of the centers, with the objective of reaching the goal in 10 years. The provincial and local governments have the responsibility of paying the costs of planning, staffing, and operating the centers. The program is now in its sixth year, and the ratio of centers to population (based on the model) has reached 1/100,000. In order to achieve the desired number of facilities by the end of the tenth year, the equivalent of 156 of these "model centers" has to be funded each year. The budget for the current year has allocated A$7,800,000 for this purpose. This will have to be increased by 15%, of course, if inflation is to be taken into account.

Roles 71–80: Representatives of the Wildlife Protection Service

The responsibility of this governmental agency is to protect the wildlife of Atlantis. In order to attain this objective, the service engaged in field operations and data collection (A$1 million), research and data analysis (A$250 thousand), outreach (conference sponsorship, radio-TV messages (A$250 thousand), and habitat acquisition (A$1.5 million for current year and each year for the past 10 years) ("A$" = Atlantis dollars). The mission of the service, which is responsible for wild birds, endangered species, and certain marine mammals, is to conserve, protect, and enhance wildlife and their habitats for the continuing benefit of the people of Atlantis.

Activities include:

- Biological monitoring, through scientific research; surveillance of pesticides and thermal pollution; studies of wildlife populations; and ecological studies;

- Environment impact assessment through river basin studies, including hydroelectric dams, nuclear power sites, and stream channelization;

- Area planning and preservation involving river basins and wilderness areas;

- Agency is responsible for improving and maintaining wildlife resources by proper management of migratory birds and other wildlife and control of population imbalances.

Table 11: Budget Proposal for the Wildlife Protection Service

(A$ = Atlantis Dollars)

	Appropriated for Current Year	Agency Recommended Budget for Next Year
Operating Costs		
Field operations and data collection	A$1,000,000	A$1,150,000*
Research and data analysis	250,000	287,500*
Outreach (conference sponsorship, radio-TV messages)	250,000	287,500*
Habitat Acquisition (each year for past 10 years)	1,500,000	1,725,000*
Total cost of operations and habitat acquisition	A$3,000,000	A$3,450,000*
Increase permitted for next year by the administration (10%)†	300,000	
Total authorized continuation budget	A$3,300,000	A$3,300,000
Shortage		A$ 150,000

*Adjusted for 15% inflation.
†The administration projects a 10% growth in tax revenues for next year and has instructed each agency to prepare a "continuation budget" which is limited to current expenditures plus 10%.

Role 81: Chair, Budget Committee; Roles 82–87: The Budget Committee Members

You should understand that the Budget Committee has the authority to do anything it wants to in dealing with an agency's request for funds. For example, the Budget Committee

1. does not have to give an agency a 10% increase in funds next year just because the administration has indicated that tax rev-

enues are expected to increase by that amount. The Budget Committee can recommend that an agency receive no increase over the current year's funds, or it can grant an amount greater than 10%.

2. may recommend that a particular agency's budget be severely cut, or even eliminated.

3. must decide what new programs, if any, should be funded.

The "bottom line" (if you can forgive that bit of accounting jargon) for the Budget Committee is that the total of all the budget recommendations for next year can be no greater than last year's total plus 10%. And there you have today's example of trying to fit a square peg into a round hole. You will find a Work Sheet on page 123. It provides you with a summary of the budget totals by agency. You may find it helpful.

Stage Three: Running the Simulation

NOTE: A brief explanation of the principles of Parliamentary Procedure is located in the Appendix. You will find especially useful for reference during the simulation run the Rank Order of Commonly Used Motions (p. 219) and the Sequence of Motions chart (p. 219).

When your instructor announces that the simulation will begin, all the agency representatives will move to locations designated by your instructor. The members of each agency will at once select one of their members to be agency chief and a second to be associate agency chief.

Meanwhile, the Budget Committee will assemble in front of the class, with the Chair of the committee located in the middle of the group. The Chair of the Budget Committee should at once appoint a secretary for the committee. The secretary will keep a record *only of actions taken* by the committee. Thus no record will be kept of who said what. *All motions will be recorded* as soon as they are introduced, plus a record of what results (such as amendments, postponements, approval, defeat, etc.).

The Budget Committee has three tasks:

- First, it will hold a hearing on the eight remaining agency budget proposals. As stated earlier, any member of the Budget Committee may ask questions about the budget being discussed; an agency chief (or, in case of absence, the associate chief) may request an opportunity to explain a particular budget. Your instructor will advise the Budget Committee of whatever time constraints are to be imposed on the hearing portion of the process.

- The second task for the Budget Committee members is to discuss among themselves how to deal with the requests for funds and yet remain within the constraints imposed by the President. This discussion will take place in front of the class. While this public decision making of a Budget Committee (which is actually a committee acting for the President) may be somewhat unrealistic, it is essential for everyone to observe how the Budget Committee deals with this allocation problem. Once again, your instructor will advise the Budget Committee of any time constraints.

- Finally, the Budget Committee must make its decisions. These actions also will be done publicly. A simple majority of those voting on the issue is all that is required to approve a budget request or any aspect of it.

The actual procedure for carrying out the preceding tasks is as follows:

The simulation will begin when the Chair of the Budget Committee calls the meeting to order. He will state:

''The Budget Committee is called to order and the first order of business is a review of the funding requests for next year of the following agencies:

- The Abortion Clinics Program

- The Crisis Centers Program

- The Day-Care Centers Program

- The Marine Safety Rescue Service

- The National Parks Service

- The Scholarships for College Students Program

- The Senior Citizens Center Program

- The Wildlife Protection Service

We will consider each of these agency requests separately. Does any member of the Budget Committee wish to ask a question or comment on any aspect of the Abortion Clinics Program?''

When the questions have ended, the Chair will state:

''Does the agency chief or any representative of the Abortion Clinics Program wish to make a comment or ask a question?''

When the questions or comments have ended, the Chair will then state:

''Next, we will review the funding request for the Crisis Centers Program. Does any member of the Budget Committee wish to comment on any aspect of this program?''

When the questions or comments have ended, the Chair will state:

''Does the agency chief or any representative of the Crisis Centers Program wish to make a comment or ask a question?''

A similar format will be used for each of the remaining funding requests.

At the conclusion of the review of the funding requests of all eight agencies, the Chair will state:

''The hearing is ended. The Budget Committee will now discuss the several proposals, searching for ways to meet the constraints imposed by the President. Does any member of the Budget Committee wish to suggest where revisions could or should be made?''

This discussion will continue until time runs out.

The Budget Committee must now make its decisions about how to bring the requests into line with the amount authorized by the President. The best way to handle that is for a member of the Budget Committee to recommend an amount for a particular agency in the form of a motion. For example:

MEMBER: ''Mr. Chairman (or Madam Chairwoman)''

CHAIR: ''Mr. Jones (or Ms. Jones)''

MEMBER: ''I move that the budget for next year for the mass transit system in the province of Omega be A\$250,000.''

MEMBER: ''Second the motion.''

CHAIR: ''It has been moved and seconded that the budget for the mass transit system in the province of Omega be A\$250,000. Is there any discussion?''

The Budget Committee may want to refer to the Appendix to refresh its memories on Rank Order of Commonly Used Motions. A simple majority of those voting on the issue is required to pass such a motion as the one above.

The Budget Committee will be warned that it must complete its voting on all the budget proposals at a time prescribed by your instructor.

Stage Four: Debriefing and Critique

Your instructor will inform you when this is to begin.

NOTE: Your instructor may ask you to complete and turn in the Evaluation Form which can be found following the page of Income Distribution Tables.

Table 12: Population Distribution by Income Categories

(Totals rounded to nearest hundred)
Population by Income Categories

Province	Poverty (10%)	Minimum Maintenance	Middle	Comfortable	Affluent	Total Population
Alpha	1,834,000 (8.6%)	3,369,900 (15.8%)	9,124,600 (42.8%)	4,621,900 (21.7%)	2,370,600 (11.1%)	21,321,000 (24.9%)
Beta	1,819,300 (8.6%)	3,342,800 (15.8%)	9,051,000 (42.8%)	4,584,500 (21.7%)	2,351,400 (11.1%)	21,149,000 (24.7%)
Gamma	1,496,700 (8.6%)	2,750,300 (15.8%)	7,446,200 (42.8%)	3,771,300 (21.7%)	1,934,500 (11.1%)	17,399,000 (20.3%)
Delta	1,308,600 (8.6%)	2,404,600 (15.8%)	6,510,200 (42.8%)	3,298,200 (21.7%)	1,691,400 (11.1%)	15,213,000 (17.8%)
Omega	2,099,200 (20%)	5,248,000 (50%)	2,099,200 (20%)	839,700 (8%)	209,900 (2%)	10,496,000 (12.3%)
Total	8,557,800 (10%)	17,115,600 (20%)	34,231,200 (40%)	17,115,600 (20%)	8,557,800 (10%)	85,578,000 (100%)

NOTE: Income percentages are approximate for Alpha, Beta, Gamma and Delta due to rounding to nearest hundred.

Work Sheet

	Appropriated for Current Year	Agency Recommended Budget for Next Year	Budget Committee Recommendation for Next Year
Abortion Clinics Program	A$ 3,303,250	A$ 10,910,798	
Crisis Centers Program	5,004,000	7,824,000	
Day-Care Centers Program	96,429,862	110,894,341	
Marine Safety Rescue Service	242,500	278,875	
National Parks Service	13,500,000	42,650,000	
College Scholarship Program	11,996,875	14,513,431	
Senior Citizens Centers Program	7,800,000	8,970,000	
Wildlife Protection Service	3,000,000	3,450,000	
Total appropriated for current year	141,276,487		
Total agency recommended budget for next year		199,491,445	
Increase permitted for next year by the admin. (10%)	14,127,649		
Total authorized continuation budget	A$155,404,136	A$155,404,136	
Shortage		A$ 44,087,309	

Evaluation Form **Simulation Five**

1. In comparison with other courses, or portions of courses, which you have taken, how would you rate this simulation experience?

2. What do you consider to be the most important thing (or things) you learned from the simulation?

3. Was there anything about the simulation which you found disappointing?

4. Do you have any suggestions as to how the simulation might be improved?

5. Suppose a friend had a choice of introductory American Government sections, one of which used simulations such as the one you just experienced. The friend asks you whether he or she should choose the section offering the simulation. What would your advice be?

Please indicate whether your role was:

_____ Very active (Budget Committee chair, Budget Committee member, agency spokesperson, outspoken agency person.)

_____ Moderately active (Spoke once or twice, but was not very involved.)

_____ Slightly active (Active only within the delegation discussion.)

_____ Inactive (Observed the events. Did not really participate in them.)

If more space is needed, the opposite side of this page may be used. If you wish to suggest changes or improvements in the simulation, please do so. Thank you.

S I M U L A T I O N 6

Appropriating Scarce Resources

The Legislator's Dilemmas

> *You spend a billion dollars here, and a billion dollars there, and pretty soon, you're talking about real money.*
>
> Senator Everett Dirksen

Introduction

Examination of the lengthy processes of budget making and appropriation was begun in Simulation Five, which focused on the initiation and development of the budget. A budget, as the term is employed in the United States, is a detailed proposal that recommends expenditure amounts and purposes for the forthcoming fiscal period. But it is a recommendation only; in and of itself it authorizes no expenditures of any kind. A second stage, the appropriation stage, is necessary to complete the process by which spending decisions are made by government. The simulation in the following pages turns our attention to that appropriation stage.

Your instructor may have chosen to omit Simulation Five, "The Budget Making Process," and so a repetition of some pertinent sections is provided below as necessary background information for you. Your instructor will advise you whether the following indented paragraphs are to be studied, reviewed, or omitted.

Today in the United States the preparation of a budget (i.e., the preparation of a list of proposed expenditures for the coming fiscal year, broken down agency-by-agency and activity-by-activity within each agency) is viewed as an executive branch function, but it was not always thus. Early budget making was in the hands of legislative assemblies for only they had the power to appropriate money. Later, as governments increased the number and the scope of their activities, budget making became a responsibility of the executive branch. There were several reasons for the shift of responsibility for the budget. First, the operations of administrative departments and bureaus produced a firsthand awareness of problems, of needs for responses to the problems, and of existing programs and policies. Second the expertise to design useful responses to the problems very often was to be found within the bureaus of the executive branch. Third, the pyramidal (hierarchical) structure of the executive branch permitted hard decisions and reconciliation of conflicting views to be funnelled to one location, the desk of the chief executive. Thus it was that Congress in 1921 transferred the task of making the budget to the President—one of the most significant shifts in the balance of power in the history of the republic.

One often has the feeling from contact with American radio, television, newspapers and magazines, that the struggle for appropriations is between the contending forces of the heartless versus the treasonous. The arguments seem to be based on the assumption that the trade-offs are between the suffering poor and essential defense programs. Thus, if only an "unneeded" and probably all-too-soon-obsolete weapons system could be cut from the budget, there would be money enough for all the needy. The converse argument proposes that all the alleged needy aren't really suffering that much and what should be done is to cut such programs to the bone, protecting those truly in need, while beefing up our defenses so as to protect our country. It is easy to forget that there is much hyperbole ("hype" in advertising jargon) in all this argument. Every bureaucratic agency sees its role as having an importance factor ranging from essential to vital for national survival. This is true of city, state or federal agencies—even university agencies. The job of each agency chief is to argue persuasively and to struggle as aggressively as possible to help the agency do a better job. Thus the army will always need more and better weapons, more soldiers, and better pay in order to retain high quality personnel. The air force needs better, faster, more advanced planes, and more rockets; the navy needs more ships, and so on. Likewise, agencies concerned for the needy will always want to reach out to help more of those in need, and society constantly will identify more groups in need.

Yet the struggle is not merely between compassion and defense. Less altruistic factors are also at work. Aid for the needy has consequences for nursing homes, social workers, doctors, nurses, hospitals, the drug industry, and some insurance companies. Aid for defense means large sums for aircraft manufacturers, labor unions, plus all those support industries which prosper when workers have money to spend. The local tavern and the local independent grocer also have a stake in ensuring the continued prosperity of the local defense plant, shipyard, army base, or veterans' hospital.

We must not forget that behind the very real ideological conflict of defense versus human needs is the equally important struggle between those who benefit and those who pay. At the level of state politics, for example, where defense needs are not an issue, the conflicts over budget allocations are just as intense. College students attending publicly supported universities (and university faculty, staff, and administrators) are engaging in an identical activity when they ask for more aid for higher education. At whose expense? Since most states cannot go into debt, the state leaders must make hard choices: raise taxes or give program A more than program B. Who benefits? Who loses? If colleges get more subsidy, enabling students to attend for less tuition, then that lowered cost to students is being paid by someone else.

For this simulation, the problem has been simplified, but it is not simple. You will not have to choose between national defense and human needs, nor with the problem of who pays. But you will encounter some difficult questions of who should benefit in what way. As with city and state political leaders, your task will be to make choices from among the competing demands for human needs and services.

As you approach this simulation it may be useful to bear in mind a few questions. First, is it difficult or is it easy for a legislative body to develop a priority system to guide its decisions on appropriation matters? What priorities are used in the simulation? How are they derived or developed?

Second, what is the importance of incrementalism—of starting with the current year's appropriation and perhaps adding marginal amounts to reflect changing circumstances next year? One alternative approach to budgeting is called zero-based budgeting. Instead of taking this year's budget as given and then asking whether next year's budget should be increased, decreased, or held at the same level (i.e., incrementalism), zero-based budgeting starts with a clean slate. The wisdom of continuing the agency or the program is challenged, and justification for the continuation is an essential part of the budget-making process for next year's expenditures. Which approach characterizes the simulation?

Third, is it difficult or is it easy to enlarge one appropriation by reducing another? When resources are finite, do dollar amounts get moved around from one category to another with ease? It should be observed in this connection that U.S. federal budget making is somewhat open-ended because of the ability of the federal government to borrow, to incur deficit financing. (But note that eventually the size of the federal deficit can become a concern, as it has since 1982, even though a President is not constrained as is the typical state governor, who is forbidden by the state constitution to propose any deficit whatsoever.)

Fourth, is it difficult or is it easy to accommodate new functions and organizations? What happens when a worthy new objective or organization comes onto the budget-making scene? As you think about possible answers to these questions, and as you apply the questions to the activities of the simulation, it is our hope and expectation that you will come to a fuller understanding of the appropriation process and its problems.

The simulation of the budget-making process in Simulation Five carried students through the executive branch stage. The President's Budget Committee performed its difficult task of remaining within the constraint imposed by the President of keeping expenditures next year within the projected 10% increase in tax revenues. The Budget Committee was required to decide which of the many activities of the eight different agencies and which of their pressing claims for increased funds should be supported. But that was only the first stage of the lengthy process of making spending decisions. The Budget Committee received its authority from the President of Atlantis, but now the representatives of the people of Atlantis must have their say. The President and the Budget Committee respond to their own perception of the national interest, the "big picture," modified by agency pressures. In practice, bureaucratic goals often will dominate. This is not to imply that bureaucratic goals run counter to the public interests; we mean only that the public has had little chance to influence the budget process. It is the legislature which is closer to the public, the voters. Bureaucrats don't have to run for reelection; legislators do. Not surprisingly, then, legislators tend to listen more attentively than bureaucrats when there is a public clamor for (or against) a particular program. Thus it is that legislators may not agree with the needs and priorities expressed by administrative agencies. The constituency of an agency is people who are directly affected by agency activities, typically the users of a service, or the beneficiaries of an agency program. A legislator's constituency, on the other hand, includes all the people or at least all the voters of a particular geographic area.

The Simulation

Stage One: The Issue

The problem of dividing up scarce resources is now in the hands of the Atlantis National Assembly. The entire class will participate in this simulation, with each person representing one or another of the provinces. Your instructor will indicate how many representatives there will be for each province and tell you to which provincial delegation you belong. The delegations may be of different sizes or of equal size. Your instructor will inform you. One of you will be identified as the Speaker of the House.

The legislative appropriation process is considerably more complicated than the simulation. It would be quite impossible to simulate that complexity, for the amount of time needed to run such a simulation would be prohibitive, and the participants would need to spend many weeks learning all the facts needed. It is, however, important for you to understand what has been omitted in this simplification of the stages of the legislative appropriation process. For example:

1. In the U.S. House of Representatives each representative represents a particular geographic district. Thus congressional districts are approximately equal in population but vary greatly in land area. In the Atlantis simulation, we have assumed that all the representatives from a particular province are elected at large. This reduces the complexity of interests and alignments.

2. The review of the budget requests by the Appropriations Committee of the U.S. House of Representatives is an essential stage of the American legislative process. Unfortunately, there

simply is not enough time for us to have an equivalent committee review stage prior to action by the whole house. In addition, there would be almost nothing for the rest of the class to do while our appropriations committee made its deliberations. Therefore, the simulation has assumed that the Appropriations Committee of the National Assembly already has completed its work. Your instructor will provide you with the needed budget information.

3. A third complicating factor present in the U.S. legislative process, but omitted from this simulation, is the presence and activity of political parties. Most observers agree that political parties play a role of declining influence on the American political scene. However, it would be quite wrong to say that political parties are irrelevant, especially in the operation of Congress and of the House of Representatives in particular, where the activity of party continues to be of considerable importance in maintaining discipline and cohesion among the members. However, for this simulation, the addition of political parties seemed needlessly complicating. A prime objective of the simulation is to introduce to you some of the difficulties which underlie the appropriation process—the temptation to use shortcuts such as incrementalism, and the political pressures and realities which cause conflict.

Stage Two: Running the Simulation

NOTE: A brief explanation of the principles of Parliamentary Procedure is located in the Appendix. You will find especially useful for reference during the simulation run the Rank Order of Commonly Used Motions (p.219) and the Sequence of Motions chart (p.219).

When your instructor announces that the simulation will begin, all the representatives will move to locations designated by your instructor. It will be useful for the representatives from each province to get to know each other and *to discuss whether there is a particular stake for their province in any of the budget items.* (A maximum of 10 minutes will be allowed for this.) *Each represent-*

ative should read very carefully the description of the provinces, especially his or her own province. Then each person should think through and discuss with the other representatives from the same province each of the budget proposals presented to the assembly. Remember you are an independently elected representative. Thus, no person has any better claim to speak for the entire province than you do.

Background information for each of the programs in the budget will be found in Budget Information for Simulation Six. You will need to be acquainted with that information in order to function effectively as a legislator acting on behalf of yourself and your constituents. You may find it helpful to use the Work Sheet for this simulation as the assembly discusses the proposed appropriations for the several agencies.

The simulation will begin when the Speaker calls the House to order. The Speaker will state:

"The Assembly will now come to order. The first order of business for the House is to consider the recommendations of the President (i.e., the Budget Committee) concerning the funding requests for next year for the following agencies:

- Abortion Clinics Program   pp. 138–39
- Crisis Centers Program   pp. 139–43
- Day-Care Centers Program   pp. 144–45
- Marine Safety Rescue Service   pp. 145–48
- National Parks Service   pp. 148–51
- Scholarships for College Students Program   pp. 151–55
- Senior Citizens Program   pp. 156–57
- Wildlife Protection Service   pp. 157–58
- Art Museum Program   pp. 158–59

NOTE: If your instructor has chosen to modify this list, you and the Speaker will have been informed.)

"We will consider each of these agency requests separately. The floor is now open for debate on the Abortion Clinics Program. According to the Rules of the Assembly, debate will be limited to 10 minutes on this issue. Motions to amend, if desired, are in order. At the end of 10 minutes, or sooner if the Assembly desires, we will vote on the Abortion Clinics Program budget request.'' (It should be noted that even though the Assembly will vote on the Abortion Clinics Program at the end of 10 minutes, it may reconsider this vote at any time until the final vote is taken on all the eight agencies.)

When the Assembly has voted on the Abortion Clinics Program, the Speaker will then state:

''We will now consider the funding request for the Crisis Centers Program. The floor is open for debate on this issue. I remind you that debate is limited to 10 minutes. A vote on this issue will be taken at the end of that time.''

A similar format will be used for each of the remaining funding requests. (If class time runs out before all the funding requests have been considered, the Speaker will ask for a motion to recess the Assembly until the next class meeting.)

At the conclusion of the debate and voting on each of the agency funding requests, the Speaker will announce if the total requests are within the mandated maximum amount. If not, then additional amounts must be deleted from the funding requests to meet that objective.)

Members of the Assembly may want to refer to the Appendix of the *Atlantis* text to refresh their memories on Rank Order of Commonly Used Motions. A simple majority of those voting on the issue is required to pass the motions you will use in this simulation.

Stage Three: Debriefing and Critique

At a time prescribed by your instructor, the simulation will end and the debriefing and critique will begin.

NOTE: Your instructor may ask you to complete and turn in the evaluation form located at the end of Budget Information for Simulation Six.

Budget Information for Simulation 6

Abortion Clinics Program

Background Information

The issue in Atlantis is not the permissibility of abortion. That has come to be accepted as a matter of personal conscience, and a majority of the people support this view. What remains controversial is the issue of public funding of abortion, which in effect exacts support both from those who approve abortion and from those who oppose it on moral grounds.

Current practice fully funds abortion on demand for any woman whose family income is below the minimum maintenance level. This may appear as a fairly straightforward issue, but there are two complicating factors. The first of these is the difference in the percentage of those in the poverty category: Alpha, Beta, Gamma, Delta—8.6%; Omega—20%.

The second factor is the difference in the cultural attitudes toward abortion. Omegans are very conservative, and only 1% of the women who are in households below the median income and who are of childbearing age (16–40) have an abortion in a given year. Alpha and Gamma are somewhat less conservative than Omega, and 2% of the women below median income and of childbearing age seek abortions in any one year. The least conservative province, as one might expect, is Beta. Perhaps surprising to some, Delta, while it is culturally quite unlike Beta, has a similarly high rate of abortion—10% for women of childbearing age from households below the median income.

Here are some facts the Assembly will need in order to make its recommendations:

1. The cost of an abortion is A$50. (A$ = Atlantis dollars.) The 15% inflation rate will increase this to A$57.50 next year.

2. Public funding for abortions this year totaled A$3,303,250. This amount covered the cost of abortions for all women in the poverty income category, and it takes into account the differential rates of poverty income levels and abortion in the provinces.

3. The Abortion Clinics Program leadership has proposed that for next year the staff of the clinics be enlarged so that all women in the minimum maintenance income category will be

able to have abortions fully paid with public funds. This will require an additional A$7,112,060 (adjusted for 15% inflation). The figure takes into account the differential rates of minimum maintenance levels and abortions in the provinces.

Table 13: Budget Proposal for the Abortion Clinics Program

(A$ = Atlantis Dollars)	Appropriated for Current Year	Agency Recommended Budget for Next Year	Budget Committee Recommendation
Abortions requested by women in poverty income level. Full funding. (66,065)†	A$3,303,250	A$3,798,738*	A$1,651,625
Abortions requested by women in minimum maintenance income level. Full funding. (123,688)†	— 0 —	7,112,060*	
Total subsidy for abortion clinics	A$3,303,250	A$10,910,798	A$1,651,625§
Increase permitted for next year by the administration (10%)‡	330,325		
Total authorized continuation budget	A$3,633,575	A$3,633,575	A$3,633,575
Difference between continuation budget and agency request (Shortfall)		A$7,277,223	
Expenditures proposed by Budget Committee: Less than continuation budget—creates a surplus of			A$1,981,950

*Adjusted for 15% inflation.
†Takes into account differential abortion rates in the provinces.
‡The administration projects a 10% growth in tax revenues for next year and has instructed each agency to prepare a "continuation budget" which is limited to current expenditures plus 10%.
§Program to be reduced by 50%.

Crisis Centers Program

Background Information

Some years ago, the national government began funding crisis centers. Identification of the need for such centers grew out of the women's movement, a factor in the politics of Atlantis as it was in the United States. The program was very modest in its early years, consisting primarily of just a few centers located in the largest cities. The usefulness of these initial efforts in assisting female victims of assault and rape led to demands for the establishment of centers throughout Atlantis.

The activities of the centers are mostly those of a counseling and advising nature. Thus the centers have no medical facilities but serve rather as a referral agency to make sure the victims of rape are admitted to a hospital familiar with the evidentiary aspects of the problem and that the police are alerted that a crime has been committed. Rape victims often do not know where to go or what to do in order to receive both proper medical assistance and to assist the police and the prosecutor in gathering evidence against an accused rapist. Thus the centers have developed cooperative procedures so that the victim is cared for, the needed photographic and medical evidence is collected immediately, and the police are assisted (and prodded, when necessary) in their efforts to find the rapist. Other activities include psychological counseling for women victims of domestic violence, especially when inflicted by a relative or spouse. Referrals in this case involve the identification of appropriate relief agencies to find housing, medical care if needed, and/or sources of assistance in cases where the victim is faced with such problems as suddenly being alone, without funds, without skills, perhaps even with suicidal tendencies, and perhaps with young children.

Crisis centers are now located throughout Atlantis, but the number of such centers varies considerably from province to province. The primary reason for this is not political, but the financial realities caused by variations in population density. Where population is concentrated in a number of large cities, as it is on Alpha and Beta, it is much simpler to reach the affected individuals, for very few women live far from a crisis center. But where there are many small towns scattered throughout the countryside, as on Gamma, Delta, and Omega, the problem becomes quite difficult to solve. To establish a center in every little town would be a prohibitively expensive undertaking; to establish them only in major cities would mean that some women would never be able to get to a center. An unhappy, but perhaps realistic, compromise was reached, and what is called the ''model center''* ratio was established. This ''model center'' should not be viewed as an ideal, but rather as an adequate minimum. Here are the facts the House will need to know:

1. A "model center" is used as a funding model. The concept is used to describe the resources and the costs of a center which would serve a typical city of 100,000 persons. The costs incorporated by the model then become the basis for calculating the national government's contribution to the provincial government for support of a crisis center. The provincial government is free, if it chooses, to add funds, to broaden the scope of service, to establish more centers, etc. But the Atlantis contribution is determined by a combination of the model cost and the ratio of centers to population in that province, which enables one to calculate how many "model centers" the province is entitled to receive from the Atlantis government. (See #4 below.) A "model center" has a staff of two professionals and one clerk-secretary-receptionist.

2. The cost of this "model center" is A\$9,000 per year (personnel—A\$6,000; office operations—A\$3,000). Adjusted for 15% inflation, this figure will be A\$10,350.

3. This "model center" staff has been found to be adequate to meet the demands for assistance of women who are victims of rape or domestic violence.

4. The population ratios that have been used to determine how many "centers" (i.e., how many center equivalents) each province is entitled to, how many staff they will be authorized, are as follows:

	Ratio of centers to population
Alpha and Beta—70% urbanized NOTE: This means that the goal is to have no more than 5% of the population beyond 80 kilometers (50 miles) range of some center; that is, 95% of the population is within 80 kilometers (50 miles) of a center.	1/100,000
Gamma and Delta—50% urbanized NOTE: This means that the goal is to have no more than 15% of the population beyond 100 kilometers (62 miles) range of some center; that is, 85% of the population is within 100 kilometers (62 miles) of a center.	1/300,000
Omega—30% urbanized NOTE: No distance criterion has been established.	1/500,000

5. The estimate is that a "model center" will be able to deal with about 700 cases per year of women in need of counseling, referral, and follow up because of rape or domestic violence.

Now, however, the crisis centers are facing several types of criticism. Too many women are simply unable to receive assistance in the provinces where low population density has brought about the use of larger ratios, resulting in fewer centers, both absolutely and relatively. In addition, many women must travel quite far in order to receive such assistance as is available.

Minimal assistance is currently available for child victims of sexual assault or physical violence. Only recently have centers been trying to help child victims, and this has created work loads for the staff far beyond what they have either the time or the expertise to handle. It is quite apparent, for example, that each "model center" should include the expertise of a child psychologist in addition to the two professionals in each "center."

No provision has ever been made to address the problem of male victims. While not numerous, male victims of domestic violence are nevertheless appearing in increasing numbers at the centers. The assailant may be the spouse, an adult child, or a rela-

Table 14: Comparison of Number of Crisis Centers Produced by Using Existing Ratios versus the Proposed Ratios

	Existing Ratios Number of "Model Centers"*	Proposed Ratios Number of "Model Centers"
Alpha	213 (1/100,000)	213 (1/100,000)
Beta	211 (1/100,000)	211 (1/100,000)
Gamma	60 (1/300,000)	87 (1/200,000)
Delta	51 (1/300,000)	76 (1/200,000)
Omega	21 (1/500,000)	53 (1/200,000)
Total Number of Centers	556	640

*The "model center" concept is a way of planning costs, not necessarily an actual center. Thus Alpha's 213 "centers" mean it is authorized the equivalent of 213 × A$9,000, or A$1,917,000. Actual location of the centers, determination of the number of such centers in the province, and the staff size in a particular center are administrative matters.

tive. In one case, a severely beaten man had been victimized by his wife and daughter. Since the centers have neither the mandate nor staff to handle such cases, all are turned away and urged to report the assault to the police.

As you will note, the proposed budget for next year proposes several increases to meet the cost of these new services.

Table 15: Budget Proposal for the Crisis Centers Program

(A$ = Atlantis Dollars)	Appropriated for Current Year	Agency Recommended Budget for Next Year	Budget Committee Recommendation
"Model Centers" now established (556) (at A$9,000 each)	A$5,004,000	A$5,754,600*	
Increase of 84 "model centers" to eliminate some of the differential caused by differences in provincial population density. Gamma, Delta, and Omega would then be funded according to ratio of one "center" per 200,000 population (at A$10,350 each)	— 0 —	869,400*	
Addition of equivalent of ½ full-time child psychologist in each "model center" to meet needs of child victims. (A$1250 × 640)	— 0 —	800,000	
Addition of equivalent of ¼ full-time male case worker in each "model center" to meet the needs of male victims. (A$625 × 640)	— 0 —	400,000	
Total support Crisis Centers	A$5,004,000	A$7,824,000	A$3,335,700†
Increase permitted for next year by administration (10%)	500,400‡		
Total authorized continuation budget	A$5,504,400	A$5,504,400	A$5,504,000
Difference between continuation budget and budget request (shortfall)		A$2,319,600	
Expenditures proposed by Budget Committee: Less than continuation budget—creates a surplus of			A$2,168,700

*Adjusted for 15% inflation.
†All growth eliminated and existing programs reduced by one-third.
‡The administration projects a 10% growth in the revenues for next year and has instructed each agency to prepare a "continuation budget" which is limited to current expenditures plus 10%.

Day-Care Centers Program

Background Information

Atlantis has experienced a phenomenon familiar to Americans: large numbers of preschool age children have both parents working or a single parent who works. The demand for and use of day-care centers has grown very rapidly. Yet the cost of this service is not cheap. Here are some facts the House members must consider:

1. Annual cost of operations of a typical day-care center, serving a maximum of 23 children:

One professional	A$1,200
Two aides at A$600	1,200
Supplies, rent, utilities, etc.	1,000
Total annual cost of operations of a typical center	A$3,400
(A$ = Atlantis dollars)	

2. For the past four years the Atlantis government has been funding either some portion or all of the cost of day-care centers for children of needy families. Families pay different amounts for day care of a child, depending on family income. The actual cost per child for 12 months of day care averages out to A$150. Thus this is the amount supplied for children whose family income is at the poverty income level. Half that amount (A$75) on average is provided to children whose family income is at the minimum maintenance level; one-quarter of that amount (A$37.50) is provided for those whose family income is below the median income level. (Adjusted for inflation, these figures will be A$172.50; A$86.50; and A$43.13.)

3. As you would expect, not all mothers or fathers with eligible children will use day-care centers. Unemployable parents will have no need for a day-care center. Some parents will be concerned for the safety of their children or about the quality of the care and nurture at the center. Some parents will prefer to leave their children with grandparents or other relatives. Because of the difficulty of travel to the center, some parents will find it easier to keep the children at home.

4. For the purposes of this simulation, it is assumed that, proportionate to population, there is uniform distribution throughout the provinces of children in need of day-care services.

5. The number of children attending government day-care centers, according to subsidy levels, are:

Income Level	Number of Children
Full funding (Poverty Level Income)	367,352
Half funding (Minimum Maintenance Income Level)	440,822
Quarter funding (Income Below Median)	220,411

Table 16: Budget Proposal for the Day-Care Centers Program

(A$ = Atlantis Dollars)	Appropriated for Current Year	Agency Recommended Budget for Next Year	Budget Committee Recommendation
Full funding of poverty level	A$55,102,800	A$63,368,220*	
Half funding of minimum maintenance level	33,061,650	38,020,897*	
Quarter funding of those with income below the median	8,265,412	9,505,224*	
Total cost of program	A$96,429,862	A$110,894,341	A$106,072,848‡
Increase permitted for next year by the administration (10%)†	9,642,986		
Total authorized continuation budget	A$106,072,848	A$106,072,848	A$106,072,848
Difference between continuation budget and agency budget (shortfall)		A$4,821,493	

*Adjusted for 15% inflation.
†The administration projects a 10% growth in tax revenues for next year and has instructed each agency to prepare a "continuation budget" which is limited to current expenditures plus 10%.
‡Current year's appropriation plus 10%.

Marine Safety and Rescue Service

Background Information

One of the earliest traditions on the islands which came to be known as Atlantis was the Marine Safety and Rescue Service. The rescue service dates back to the time before the provinces were officially established by the United Nations and when population was thinly settled along the coastlines. Not surprisingly, shipping was an important activity, and it became a matter of great pride for the citizens of the small coastal towns to volunteer to take part in the rescue of passengers and crews of ships in distress. Numerous potential victims of storms were saved by the brave volunteer rescue crews, and many local heroes found their niche in local history. Local legends are replete with the tales of vicious storms, great courage and tragic deaths.

The local volunteer crews and the marine stations which sponsor them still perform important services. Classes are held on the development of basic skills of seamanship, there are free schools on watercraft safety and navigation, and all this is done by the volunteers. Marine Rescue Days, as they are called, continue to be held as an annual celebration and the rescue boats compete to bring honor to their towns, to break records, and to immortalize the crews. As a result of all these activities, the Marine Safety and Rescue Service continues to have a strong political base. The local towns view Marine Rescue Days as vital to the maintenance of strong community feelings, a means of preserving an honored history while simultaneously uniting newcomers with the towns' historic residents. It is provincialism in its best sense, meaning local identity, local pride. Consequently, the towns collectively request support for the Marine Safety and Rescue Service. The total financial support is modest, but it is essential to the continuation of the service, for it pays for the equipment (the boats, the marine radio transmitter and receiver, the storage sheds), the year-round staff (to monitor weather reports and relay distress messages or reports, to maintain the equipment), and of course the expenses related to the celebration (prizes, subsidy for the annual clambake, etc.).

Fifty towns scattered throughout the five provinces maintain these rescue services. Volunteers still meet weekly to keep the boats and the crews in shape; the marine radio, though quite antiquated, continues to transmit and receive; each town still holds its annual week-long celebration. In order to perpetuate the traditions, the local volunteer crews still struggle to save the "victims of the sea," but while the storms are as frequent as ever, the crises are not, and rarely is there a victim in danger. In reality, the Marine Safety and Rescue Service is an anachronism. The actual rescuing is handled now by heavily powered and radar/sonar-guided launches and helicopters operating from regionally located bases. The Marine Safety and Rescue Service, given its long traditions, resisted the establishment of modernized, but regionally located, rescue services. Thus it was that the Atlantis Navy assumed the tasks of rescuing crews and passengers and the MSRS gradually accepted the new world in which they merely celebrated the rescues of the past. It preserved its name, its traditions, and its activities; it gave up its rescue function. But it still has a significant and strong political base.

Table 17: Budget Proposal for Marine Safety Rescue Service

(A$ = Atlantis Dollars)

	Appropriated for Current Year	Agency Recommended Budget for Next Year	Budget Committee Recommendation
Equipment maintenance†	A$ 15,000	A$ 17,250*	
Marine radio repair†	37,500	43,125*	
Personnel (year-round, 24-hour service to monitor and relay messages on marine radio)†	175,000	201,250*	
Marine Rescue Day Celebration†	15,000	17,250*	
Marinas§	— 0 —	— 0 —	A$4,000,000
Total support for Marine Safety Rescue Service	A$242,500	A$278,875*	A$4,266,750
Increase permitted for next year by administration (10%)‡	24,250		
Total authorized continuation budget	A$266,750	A$266,750	A$ 266,750
Difference between continuation budget and agency request (shortfall)		A$ 12,125	
Expenditures proposed by Budget Committee: more than continuation budget—creates a (shortfall) of			A$4,000,000

*Adjusted for 15% inflation.
†Total based on cost for 50 towns.
‡The administration projects a 10% growth in tax revenues for next year and has instructed each agency to prepare a "continuation budget" which is limited to current expenditures plus 10%.
§Recommendation for 5 marinas (one in each province) at A$800,000 each.

The budget breakdown for a "model" town rescue service is as follows:

Rescue equipment maintenance (varnish for boats, repair of boats)	A$300
Marine radio repairs	750
Personnel (year-round, 24-hour service to monitor and relay messages on marine radio) (168 hours per week x 52 weeks = 8,736 x A$.40 per hour = A$3,500)	3,500
Marine Rescue Days Celebration	300
Total	A$4,850
(A$ = Atlantis dollars)	

National Parks Service

Background Information

The National Parks Service currently administers four national parks, one each in Alpha, Beta, Gamma, and Delta. These four parks are all about the same size, with similar scales of operations. At present there is no national park in Omega; however, the budget for next year recommends that one be established.

The objectives of the park system are to administer the properties for the enjoyment and education of all the citizens of Atlantis and to protect the natural environment of the areas. The service develops and implements park management plans and staffs the areas under its administration. It relates the natural values and historical significance of each of the parks to the public through talks, tours, films, exhibits, and publications. It operates campgrounds and other visitor facilities and provides—usually through concessions—lodging, food, and transportation services.

The budget for the National Parks Service consists of two major categories (A$ = Atlantis dollars):

1. Parks Operation, which received a total of A$11 million for the current year. Since the park system generated A$2,000,000 in user fees, the net cost to the taxpayers was A$9,000,000.
2. Park Development, which received A$4.5 million for the current year. This is the fourth year of a five-year acquisition plan

to purchase land and then develop a new park in the desert-coastal area of Omega. The first year of project development cost occurs next fiscal year, which also will be the last year of land acquisition costs.

Support for the new park proposal comes from two sources. There is, as one can appreciate, extremely strong demands for the park from Omegans. Provincial pride is clearly part of the explanation, but Omegans also desire recreational and vacation facilities which are near enough to be enjoyed without great expense or travel time. Given the cold and damp climate of the settled areas

Table 18: Budget Proposal for the National Parks Service

(A$ = Atlantis Dollars)	Appropriated for Current Year	Agency Recommended Budget for Next Year	Budget Committee Recom-mendation
Parks Operations			
Education (naturalist programs, visitors' center)	A$ 1,200,000	A$ 1,380,000*	
Safety (patrolling highways, response to medical emergencies, patrolling paths in response to complaints)	1,000,000	1,150,000	
Recreation (trail path maintenance, swimming pool, golf greens, tennis courts)	1,500,000	1,725,000*	
Maintenance and service (janitorial, road repair, trash collection, water supply, sewage disposal)	7,300,000	8,395,000*	
	A$11,000,000	A$12,650,000*	A$11,000,000‖
Income from user fees (general admission, camping, golf, tennis)†	2,000,000	2,000,000	2,000,000
Total net cost of operations	A$ 9,000,000	A$10,650,000	A$ 9,000,000‖
(See ‖ note at end.)			
Park Development—Omega National Park			
Land acquisition	A$ 4,500,000	A$ 4,500,000	— 0 —
Development (this amount, plus inflation, will have to be expended for each of the next succeeding five years.)			
Public recreation facilities		A$ 4,000,000	— 0 —

(A$ = Atlantis Dollars)	Appropriated for Current Year	Agency Recommended Budget for Next Year	Budget Committee Recommendation
Water supply (deep wells, desalinization, water storage tank)		A$ 6,000,000	— 0 —
Harbor development		A$ 5,000,000	— 0 —
Roads and trails development		A$ 6,500,000	— 0 —
Airport		A$ 2,000,000	— 0 —
Sanitary sewers, sewage disposal plant		A$ 4,000,000	— 0 —
Total cost of park development	A$ 4,500,000	A$32,000,000	— 0 —
Monuments and Memorials	— 0 —	— 0 —	A$ 2,000,000‖
Total cost of operations and development	13,500,000	42,650,000	11,000,000
Total increase permitted for next year by the administration (10%)‡	1,350,000		900,000‖
Total authorized continuation budget	A$14,850,000	A$14,850,000	A$14,850,000
Difference between continuation budget and agency request (shortfall)		A$27,800,000	
Expenditures proposed by Budget Committee: less than continuation budget—creates a surplus of			A$ 2,950,000

*Adjusted for 15% inflation.

†User fees may be increased. The total fee was raised last year from A$.60 to A$.80. However, it was discovered that as fees went up, park attendance declined. This fact was verified by a survey of park visitors. The following formula should be used to estimate amount of income from increased user fees.

Per Capita Amount of Fee	Number of Visitors per year	User Fee Revenue for year
A$ .60	2,850,000	A$1,710,000
.80	2,500,000	2,000,000
1.00	2,250,000	2,250,000
1.20	2,000,000	2,400,000
1.40	1,700,000	2,380,000

‡The administration projects a 10% growth in tax revenues for next year and has instructed each agency to prepare a "continuation budget" which is limited to current expenditures plus 10%.

§NOTE: Parks operations expenses divide up as follows:

Personnel costs	55% of total
Transport (trucks, patrol cars, gas, oil, repairs)	18% of total
Supplies & Equipment (everything from toilet paper to blacktop to seedlings)	18% of total
Miscellaneous	9% of total
	100%

‖The Budget Committee recommended a 10% increase in appropriations for the cost of *park operations only*.

It also recommended that A$2,000,000 be appropriated to build monuments/memorials to honor Atlantis citizens who have received the Nobel Prize, all of whom came from Alpha and Beta. Thus A$1,000,000 for this purpose is to be appropriated for each of these two provinces.

of Omega, development of the coastal desert area, with its hot sun, would have a great attraction for the sun-starved Omegan citizens.

There is, however, one additional advantage in developing the coastal areas of the Omegan desert: the possibility of creating a tourist attraction which might tempt foreign visitors to come to Atlantis. Support for the new park, therefore, has more than a provincial base, for if foreign trade results it means the national balance of trade will benefit. It is easy to guess what will then happen. The private land proximate to the national park will begin to attract private developers—of hotels, condominiums, banks, vacation facilities, vacation homes, and on and on. The most visionary of the planners talk of a new Riviera. But none of this can occur without the start-up support.

Scholarships for College Students Program

Background Information

The primary goal of the scholarship program has been to assist needy college students. Here are some facts the Assembly members will need in order to understand how the program works and make their decisions.

1. The population of Atlantis divides itself as follows in socio-economic terms: (A$ = Atlantis dollars)

   - Poverty Level—family income below A$500

   - Minimum Maintenance Level—family income between A$500–A$1,500

   - Median Level—family income between A$1,500–A$3,500 (Actual median income is A$2,000)

   - Comfortable Level—family income between A$3,500–A$5,000

   - Affluent Level—family income above A$5,000

2. Number and percent of high school graduates who went to college last year:

Income Level	No. of H.S. Graduates Last Year	Percent Who Went to College	No. Who Went to College
Poverty	102,102	1%	1,021
Minimum Maintenance	204,204	10	20,420
Up to the Median	204,204	25	51,051
Above the Median	204,204	25	51,051
Comfortable	204,204	60	122,522
Affluent	102,102	95	96,996
Total	1,021,020		343,061

3. College costs A$500 per academic year.

4. The policy adopted for the budget for the current fiscal year provided a national planning target of full funding (A$500) for all students whose families were in the poverty level, half funding (A$250) for all students whose families were in the minimum maintenance level, and one-quarter funding (A$125) for all students whose family incomes were below the median family income level. *But the actual distribution of money was by province on the basis of population, not on the basis of the number of needy in the population.* This legislative error was brought about because of haste in the passage of the appropriation bill.

   Stated another way, for each A$1,000 increment/decrement in the allocation next year, there will be a gain/loss of:

   - 2 full scholarships (poverty level income), or

   - 4 half scholarships (minimum maintenance family income), or

   - 8 quarter scholarships (up to the median family income)

5. The current year's budget allocation had some interesting omissions which the Department of Education has tried to address in its budget proposals. No provision was made in earlier years for merit scholarships. All scholarship awards were based entirely on need. There has been extensive public criti-

cism of this, especially by citizens whose incomes, while above the median, fall below the A$3,500 mark, which is identified as the minimum "comfortable" standard of living. Their argument stresses the unfairness of a system which places all of its emphasis on need and none on the scholarly achievements of students. They do not quarrel with helping those in need, only with the absence of incentives and support for academic achievers. In order to meet this demand, next year's budget proposal includes an item of A$57,500 for 100 full scholarships to be based on merit.

It has been a matter of concern to many citizens, and to those in charge of the scholarship program, that only 1% of the high school graduates whose family income falls in the poverty level go to college. This compared with 95% of the affluent high school graduates. What is particularly regrettable about the low college attendance level of those in the poverty income group is that their standard test scores suggest that many more are qualified to go to college and might attend if more scholarships were available.

In an attempt to expand the opportunities for social mobility for talented young people, who are not fortunate enough to have affluent parents, it has been recommended that an additional 1% of the high school graduates in the poverty level category be granted full scholarships. Next year's budget includes an item of A$587,075 to fund this objective of an additional 1,021 full scholarships.

As was indicated in the "fact" section, 10% of the families in Atlantis are classified as being in the poverty level. It was on that basis that 1,021 scholarships were authorized last year. Not surprisingly, these full scholarships were divided among the five provinces on the basis of population, as follows:

Province	Percentage of Population of Atlantis	Number of Scholarships When Distribution Is Based on Population %
Alpha	24.9%	254
Beta	24.7	252
Gamma	20.3	209
Delta	17.8	181
Omega	12.3	125
Total	100.0	1,021

Obviously, the larger and more prosperous provinces heartily approved of this arrangement. What is hidden in this allocation is the assumption that poverty is distributed approximately evenly throughout the five provinces, which tends to be correct—except for Omega. In fact, that 10% poverty factor divides up quite differently: in Alpha, Beta, Gamma, and Delta 8.6% of the families live below the poverty line, in Omega the figure is 20%! As far as the Omegans are concerned, this is just one more example of blatant discrimination against them. They are arguing—demanding—that the full scholarship allocation next year reflect the actual distribution of poverty, and be as follows:

High School Graduates	Province	Poverty Percentage	No. of Persons Below Poverty Level	Number of Poverty People Eligible to Go to College
254,234	Alpha	8.6%	21,864	219
252,192	Beta	8.6	21,689	217
207,267	Gamma	8.6	17,825	178
181,742	Delta	8.6	15,630	156
125,586	Omega	20.0	25,117	251
1,021,021			102,125	1,021

The impact of this is clear. Four of the provinces are going to lose sizeable numbers of scholarships next year if Omega is given recognition for its unfortunate economic situation.

Province	No. of Scholarships Gained or (Lost)
Alpha	(35)
Beta	(35)
Gamma	(31)
Delta	(25)
Omega	126

There are several possible alternatives. One solution is to reallocate as suggested above, so that Omega's high poverty level is recognized. It seems very likely that the four original provinces will not accept this alternative gracefully. Since they are not very fond of Omega (or Omegans) anyhow, why should they make any sacrifices for them? Another solution is to continue the allocation system used this year, even though it "discriminates" against Omegans. Let the Omegans continue to accuse the other provinces of discrimination. A third solution is to increase the total number of full scholarships by 126, so that the four original provinces will not lose any scholarships, but the Omegan share will reflect its high level of poverty. The scholarship agency has opted for this alternative and included an item of A$72,450 in the budget proposed for next year to fund these additional 126 full scholarships.

Table 19: Budget Proposal for the College Scholarship Program

(A$ = Atlantis Dollars)	Appropriated for Current Year	Agency Recommended Budget for Next Year	Budget Committee Recom- mendation
Full scholarships (1,021)	A$ 510,000	A$ 587,075*	
Full scholarships to fund additional 1% poverty level (1,021)	— 0 —	587,075	
Full scholarships to be based on merit (100)	— 0 —	57,500	
Full scholarships to assist Omega (126)	— 0 —	72,450	
Half scholarships (20,420)	5,105,500	5,870,750*	
Quarter scholarships (51,051)	6,381,375	7,338,581*	
Total scholarship assistance for college students	A$11,996,875	A$14,513,431*	A$ 5,998,438‡
Increase permitted for next year by administration (10%)†	1,199,687		
Total authorized continuation budget	A$13,196,562	A$13,196,562	A$13,196,562
Difference between continuation budget and agency request (shortfall)		A$ 1,316,869	
Expenditures proposed by Budget Committee: less than continuation budget—creates a surplus of			A$ 7,198,124

*Adjusted for 15% inflation. Full scholarship increased next year to A$575, half scholarship increased to A$287.50, quarter scholarship increased to A$143.75.

†The administration projects a 10% growth in tax revenues for next year and has instructed each agency to prepare a "continuation budget" which is limited to current expenditures plus 10%.

‡The Budget Committee recommended a 50% reduction in the current year's appropriation.

Senior Citizens Program

Background Information

Only a decade or so ago, there were few government subsidized facilities in Atlantis for older people. The recreation rooms in churches were often scheduled for senior citizen activities on certain days; sometimes private social welfare agencies would sponsor such programs. Finally, responding to the political pressure of increasingly influential organizations, such as the AARP (Atlantis Association of Retired Persons), the Atlantis National Assembly passed a law which set as a goal the construction of a senior citizens center at a ratio of one center to each 50,000 population. It must be understood that the funding of the construction is based on the concept of a "model center," which for the current year costs A$50,000 (A$ = Atlantis dollars). The concept is used to describe the resources and the costs of construction of a center which would service a typical city of 50,000. The costs incorporated by the model then become the basis for calculating the national government's contribution to the provincial government,

Table 20: Budget Proposal for the Senior Citizens Centers Program

(A$ = Atlantis Dollars)	Appropriated for Current Year	Agency Recommended Budget for Next Year	Budget Committee Recommendation
Construction of Senior Citizens Centers—156 "model centers"† at A$50,000 each	A$7,800,000	A$8,970,000*	A$3,900,000§
Increase permitted for next year by the administration (10%)‡	780,000		
Total authorized continuation budget	A$8,580,000	A$8,580,000	A$8,580,000
Difference between continuation budget and agency request (shortfall)		A$ 390,000	
Expenditures proposed by Budget Committee: less than continuation budget—creates a surplus of			A$4,680,000

*Adjusted for 15% inflation.

†The "model center" concept is a way of planning costs, not necessarily an actual center.

‡The administration projects a 10% growth in tax revenues for next year and has instructed each agency to prepare a "continuation budget" which is limited to current expenditures plus 10%.

§The Budget Committee has recommended that only 78 centers be authorized, to cost A$50,000 each.

which decides on the location and the size of the actual centers.

Responsibility for the senior citizens center program has been divided up. The national government has undertaken the task of construction of the centers, with the objective of reaching the goal in 10 years. The provincial and local governments have the responsibility of paying the costs of planning, staffing, and operating the centers. The program is now in its sixth year and the ratio of centers to population (based on the model) has reached 1/100,000. In order to achieve the desired number of facilities by the end of the tenth year, the equivalent of 156 of these "model centers" has to be funded each year. The budget for the current year has allocated A$7,800,000 for this purpose. This will have to be increased by 15%, of course, if inflation is to be taken into account.

Wildlife Protection Service

Background Information

The responsibility of this governmental agency is to protect the wildlife of Atlantis. In order to attain this objective, the service engages in field operations and data collection (A$1 million), research and data analysis (A$250 thousand), outreach (conference sponsorship, radio-TV messages) (A$250 thousand), and habitat acquisition (A$1.5 million for current year and each year for the past 10 years). (A$ = Atlantis dollars.) The mission of the service, which is responsible for wild birds, endangered species, and certain marine mammals, is to conserve, protect, and enhance wildlife and their habitats for the continuing benefit of the people of Atlantis.

Activities include:

- Biological monitoring, through scientific research; surveillance of pesticides and thermal pollution; studies of wildlife populations; and ecological studies;

- Environmental impact assessment through river basin studies, including hydroelectric dams, nuclear power sites, and stream channelization;

- Area planning and preservation involving river basins and wilderness areas.

Agency is responsible for improving and maintaining wildlife resources by proper management of migratory birds and other wildlife and control of population imbalances.

Table 21: Budget Proposal for the Wildlife Protection Service

(A$ = Atlantis Dollars)	Appropriated for Current Year	Agency Recommended Budget for Next Year	Budget Committee Recom- mendation
Operating Costs			
Field operations and data collection	A$1,000,000	A$1,150,000*	A$1,000,000‡
Research and data analysis	250,000	287,500*	— 0 —
Outreach (conference sponsorship, radio-TV messages)	250,000	287,500*	— 0 —
Habitat Acquisition (each year for past 10 years)	1,500,000	1,725,000*	500,000‡
Total cost of operations and habitat acquisition	A$3,000,000	A$3,450,000*	A$1,500,000‡
Increase permitted for next year by the administration (10%)	300,000		
Total authorized continuation budget	A$3,300,000	A$3,300,000	A$3,300,000
Difference between continuation budget and agency request (shortfall)		A$ 150,000	
Expenditures proposed by Budget Committee: less than continuation budget—creates a surplus of			A$1,800,000

*Adjusted for 15% inflation.

†The administration projects a 10% growth in tax revenues for next year and has instructed each agency to prepare a "continuation budget" which is limited to current expenditures plus 10%.

‡The Budget Committee has recommended that Habitat Acquisition be reduced by A$1,000,000 and that Research/Data Analysis and Outreach be eliminated for next year. No 10% increased is authorized.

Art Museum Program

Background Information

The artistic and intellectual community of Atlantis has been urging for some time that greater recognition be given to the arts and that public support be provided to build an art museum in each of the provincial capitals. Resolutions of endorsement have been passed unanimously by each of the provincial legislatures.

The Budget Committee agrees that such a program is long overdue and has recommended that a maximum of A$3,000,000 (A$ = Atlantis dollars) be appropriated for each of the five museums. The only stipulation made by the Budget Committee, other than that each province is to receive the same allocation, is that the museums should emphasize the artistic achievements of native (i.e., citizen) artists.

Table 22: Budget Proposal for the Art Museum Program

(A$ = Atlantis Dollars)	Appropriated for Current Year	Agency Recommended Budget for Next Year	Budget Committee Recommendation
Operating Costs	— 0 —	— 0 —	— 0 —
Land acquisition and construction costs	— 0 —	— 0 —	A$15,000,000
Total authorized continuation budget	— 0 —	— 0 —	A$15,000,000
Expenditures proposed by Budget Committee: more than continuation budget—creates a (shortfall) of	— 0 —	— 0 —	(A$15,000,000)

Table 23: Population Distribution by Income Categories

(Totals rounded to nearest hundred)

Population by Income Categories

Province	Poverty	Minimum Maintenance	Middle	Comfortable	Affluent	Total Population
Alpha	1,834,000 (8.6%)	3,369,900 (15.8%)	9,124,600 (42.8%)	4,621,900 (21.7%)	2,370,600 (11.1%)	21,321,000 (24.9%)
Beta	1,819,300 (8.6%)	3,342,800 (15.8%)	9,051,000 (42.8%)	4,584,500 (21.7%)	2,351,400 (11.1%)	21,149,000 (24.7%)
Gamma	1,496,700 (8.6%)	2,750,300 (15.8%)	7,446,200 (42.8%)	3,771,300 (21.7%)	1,934,500 (11.1%)	17,399,000 (20.3%)
Delta	1,308,600 (8.6%)	2,404,600 (15.8%)	6,510,200 (42.8%)	3,298,200 (21.7%)	1,691,400 (11.1%)	15,213,000 (17.8%)
Omega	2,099,200 (20%)	5,248,000 (50%)	2,099,200 (20%)	839,700 (8%)	209,900 (2%)	10,496,000 (12.3%)
Total	8,557,800 (10%)	17,115,600 (20%)	34,231,200 (40%)	17,115,600 (20%)	8,557,800 (10%)	85,578,000 (100%)

NOTE: Income percentages are approximate for Alpha, Beta, Gamma and Delta due to rounding to nearest hundred.

Work Sheet

	Appropriated for Current Year	Agency Recommended Budget for Next Year	Budget Committee Recommendation for Next Year	Actual Appropriation of the Atlantis National Assembly
Abortion Clinics Program	A$ 3,303,250	A$ 10,910,798	A$ 1,651,625	
Crisis Centers Program	5,004,000	7,824,000	3,335,700	
Day-Care Centers Program	96,429,862	110,894,341	106,072,848	
Marine Safety Rescue Service	242,500	278,875	4,266,750	
National Parks Service	13,500,000	42,650,000	11,900,000	
College Scholarship Program	11,996,875	14,513,431	5,998,438	
Senior Citizens Centers Program	7,800,000	8,970,000	3,900,000	
Wildlife Protection Service	3,000,000	3,450,000	1,500,000	
Art Museums	— 0 —	— 0 —	15,000,000	
Total appropriated for current year	141,276,487			
Total agency recommended budget for next year		199,491,445		
Total recommended by Budget Committee for next year			153,625,361	
Increase permitted for next year by the admin. (10%)	14,127,649			
Total authorized continuation budget	A$155,404,136	A$155,404,136	A$155,404,136	
Difference between continuation budget and agency request (shortfall)		(A$ 44,087,309)		
Expenditures proposed by Budget Committee: less than continuation budget—creates a surplus of			A$ 1,778,775	

Evaluation Form Simulation Six

1. In comparison with other courses, or portions of courses, which you have taken, how would you rate this simulation experience?

2. What do you consider to be the most important thing (or things) you learned from the simulation?

3. Was there anything about the simulation which you found disappointing?

4. Do you have any suggestions as to how the simulation might be improved?

5. Suppose a friend had a choice of introductory American Government sections, one of which used simulations such as the one you just experienced. The friend asks you whether he or she should choose the section offering the simulation. What would your advice be?

Please indicate whether your role (as you played it) was:

_____ Very active (Spoke frequently.)

_____ Moderately active (Spoke once or twice, but was not very involved.)

_____ Slightly active (Spoke once or twice within provincial discussions.)

_____ Not active (Observed the events, but did not really participate in them.)

If more space is needed, the opposite side of this page may be used. If you wish to suggest changes or improvements in the simulation, please do so. Thank you.

Introduction to Simulations 7 and 8

The First Amendment: Who Needs It?

Fear of serious injury cannot alone justify suppression of free speech and assembly. Men feared witches and burnt women. It is a function of speech to free men from the bondage of irrational fears.

Justice Brandeis
Whitney v. California (1927)

The Problem

With phrases now familiar to every American, the First Amendment to the United States Constitution specifically forbids Congress to pass any law which would curtail our basic freedoms: speech, press, exercise of religion, separation of church and state, peaceful assembly, and petition. We now take these rights quite for granted; yet in 1798, only six years after the First Amendment was ratified by two-thirds of each house of Congress and by the legislatures of three-fourths of the states, Congress approved the Sedition Act, the purpose of which was to suppress and punish political opposition. Some 25 persons were prosecuted under this act, of whom 10 were convicted. Their punishment included both fines and imprisonment. What were their "crimes"? They had written denunciations of governmental leaders and policies— they had exercised the freedom of the press supposedly protected by the First Amendment. How could these incredible events have happened?

As the Founding Fathers drafted the United States Constitution in Philadelphia in 1787 they remembered vividly their experience with the tyranny of the English colonial governors. Eleven years earlier the Declaration of Independence had proclaimed a ringing denunciation of a detailed list of crimes committed by these governors against the American colonists. When the Philadelphia Convention of 1787 completed its work these guarantees of the great freedoms were omitted, the delegates supposing that a federal government limited to only those powers given by the Constitution needed no further constraint upon its scope of action; but the Framers miscalculated the public temperament. Strong guarantees were demanded by skeptics, and the Bill of Rights—the first 10 Amendments to the Constitution—was proposed to quiet the fears of the public and win acceptance for the new Constitution. In effect, the Constitution and the Bill of Rights came as a package deal. Even from today's perspective it is easy to understand why citizens wanted to prevent, for example, the passing of bills of attainder (punishment by a legislative body rather than by a court of law) or ex post facto laws (which retroactively defined as criminal conduct actions that were entirely lawful when they occurred). But of more concern to us as we consider the revision of the Atlantis Constitution is the reasoning behind the provisions of the First Amendment. Let us look, then, more carefully at that remarkable amendment.

The Framers' Solution

It is important to recall at the outset that the independence of our judiciary is at the heart of American freedoms. In colonial times the judges were appointed by the crown, or by agents of the crown in the case of the colonies. They served at the pleasure of the crown, which meant that they were subject to removal from office whenever one of their decisions incurred the displeasure of the crown (or the colonial governor). This was one of the specific complaints listed in the Declaration of Independence: "The present King of Great Britain . . . has made judges dependent on his Will alone, for the tenure of their offices, and the amount and payment of their salaries." It is not surprising that these colonial judges made their decisions with a clear understanding of who was their employer. The wording of Article III of the United States Constitution reflects the experience of the colonists when it states: "The judges, both of the supreme and inferior Courts, shall hold their Offices during good Behaviour, and shall, at stated Times, receive for their Services, a Compensation, which shall not be diminished during their Continuance in Office."

Having made the judiciary at least somewhat independent of the executive and legislative branches by insulating the judiciary from threats of firing or reduction in salary, the Constitution Framers placed in the document limitations on the suspension of the writ of habeas corpus (the writ being our most important shield against unlawful imprisonment), and they added a prohibition against bills of attainder and ex post facto laws, at which point they thought they had dealt adequately with the problem of protecting liberty. This proved to be a mistaken notion quickly seized upon by the critics of the new Constitution, as noted above, and thus the First Amendment came to be proposed. Notice, if you will, that the language of the First Amendment does not protect citizens against actions by the states, their governors, or their legislatures. Its language protects only against federal government actions. Although each state had similar provisions in the state constitution, the availability of the First Amendment as a shield against actions of state or local governments developed only in the present century as the U.S. Supreme Court interpreted the word *liberty* in the Fourteenth Amendment (an amendment arising out of the Civil War and intended to define the rights of all persons, without regard to race) so as to include at least the fundamental liberties expressed in the First Amendment. In other words, the First Amendment, limiting according to its terms only the federal government, was read into the Fourteenth Amendment and thereby became a limitation on state and local governments as well.

Thus we see how the First Amendment came into existence, but understanding its historical importance does not necessarily explain its continuing importance. To illustrate, the Constitution forbids (in the First Amendment) abridging freedom of speech or press, and it also forbids (in Article I, Section 10) granting any title of nobility. Clearly, one provision is of extraordinary importance today while the other is of no present consequence whatsoever. But why is the First Amendment so important today? To answer, we need to consider the relationship between freedom of speech and democracy.

Democracy and the First Amendment

There seems little doubt that freedom of speech is the cornerstone of a democratic society, for without such freedom the prospect for democratic accountability and for the interplay of competing ideas in the development of public policy would die. Moreover, freedom of speech is intimately related to the other freedoms of the First Amendment—freedom of religion, of press, of assembly and of petition, and without freedom of speech the others would be in great jeopardy. As anyone who has familiarity with the history of Nazi Germany or the Soviet Union can testify, control of information is fundamental to the maintenance of a dictatorial regime. Democracies depend on the unrestricted flow of information; without it they wither and die.

If democracies are indeed so dependent on the free flow of information for their survival, are they not then quite vulnerable? Though it might seem so at first glance, they are not all that fragile, for there are several good reasons for the persistence of these freedoms. In the first place, individual freedom seems to be a nearly universal goal. Perhaps it cannot be proved with certainty, but the yearning to pursue one's own preferences and one's own goals appears to be ubiquitous. Most of us regard it as a positive good whose acceptance needs no proof. It is one of life's givens. Thus freedom of speech is doubly supported—as a positive good in its own right and as an instrumental good contributing to the achievement of other goals as well.

A second reason for the durability of these freedoms is found in the writings of Seymour Martin Lipset. He starts with the fact that modern, developed democracies are by their very nature diverse, heterogeneous. In order for them to cohere and survive as societies, that diversity must be protected. This protection, in turn, can and apparently does elicit support and loyalty from the many different groups which comprise the society and which recognize the importance of the government's sheltering of diversity. An excellent example of this is religious toleration, one of the most remarkable social inventions of Western civilization. For centuries men supposed that failure to worship as did the sovereign was treason. The notion that a sovereign who sheltered diversity by permitting each to worship according to choice might attach the subjects all the more securely to the government which protected their religious freedom was slow to develop. Indeed, we see every day in our newspapers tragic evidence that many sectors of the globe perceive the notion dimly or not at all. Nevertheless, the notion did develop and catch on in many societies. (Unfortunately, the possible relationship between religious toleration and the demands of technological development, though intriguing, cannot be explored here.) By refraining from attempts to establish an official religion and by protecting all religious groups from the government and from each other the government enhances its own legitimacy; the government enhances the belief of the citizenry that the government's institutions and practices are appropriate and beneficial for the society. The lesson is quite clear; freedom of speech is the cornerstone of democracy.

This description of the importance of freedom of speech does not, however, tell us where we may find the outer limits of that freedom. There are some who argue that freedom of speech is an absolute, that there should be no restrictions placed upon it. The more widely held view is that no freedom is without limits, but then those who hold that view promptly disagree among themselves concerning the question of where the limits are to be found and by whom. Reasonable people (plus some who appear not very reasonable at all) are likely to differ substantially over the question. For example, can anyone at any time "practice" his or her religious beliefs anywhere? Can one defame another person, either orally or in writing, with impunity? Does the principle of religious freedom confer the right to sacrifice animals, or even humans, in the name of one's religion or one's freedom? What about the problem of certain political "extremists" who live in a democracy but who refuse to accept the constraints of the democratic process, examples being the Irish Republican Army, the Red Brigade in Europe, the Puerto Rican Nationalists, and others who in like fashion include indiscriminate bombing and assassination in their repertoire of "political techniques," defending their actions with assertions that the justice of their cause justifies the means they have chosen? If there is a limit, where is it located and who shall point it out?

Each of the two simulations which follow attempts to deal with the excruciating dilemma we face when we must deal with the possible limits of speech and behaviors seemingly protected by the First Amendment. Each simulation presents us with the question, where does one draw the line? Simulation Seven explores problems of the free exercise of religion and the separation of church and state (i.e. the "establishment" clause); Simulation Eight explores problems of political speech.

Dilemmas of Religious Freedom

The First Amendment versus Society's Right to Protect Its Citizens

If there is any fixed star in our constitutional constellation, it is that no official, high or petty, can prescribe what shall be orthodox in politics, nationalism, religion, or other matters of opinion, or force citizens to confess by word or act their faith thereon. If there are any circumstances which permit an exception, they do not now occur to us.

Justice Jackson
West Virginia State Board of Education v. Barnette (1943)

Introduction

Religious freedom was the goal of all the early settlers who came to American shores, for religious persecution was a common experience for all of them. Protestants, Catholics, Jews, and nonbelievers all understood how dangerous it was to life and limb to deviate from the established religion of the state. European history in the 17th century is replete with examples. So it was that when the colonists came to the new lands their goal was to make the world safe for *their* religion. It was not one of their goals to make the world safe for the religion of those who differed from them. The concept of one true faith was a widely accepted value, especially for the settlers of New England, Maryland, and Pennsylvania. Freedom of religion, not tolerance of religious differences, was the norm. Only Roger Williams of Rhode Island preached and established the notion of religious tolerance.

By the late 18th century it was apparent to those who were writing the U.S. Constitution that the diversity of religions already present in the 13 states made it impossible for a single national religion to be established. In addition, the terrible harm inflicted upon individuals and the nation by religious conflict was well known. So it was that Article VI, Sec. 3 eliminated a religious test for office (a person is required only to "affirm" willingness to support the Constitution upon accepting public office), and the First Amendment forbids Congress to abridge the exercise of religious freedom or to establish an official religion.

As stated earlier, the establishment of religious toleration as the official policy of the nation is much more than merely a nice thing to do. Granted, it may be good in and of itself to protect religious diversity and the right to have individual religious preference. But, in addition, when all religions are protected from the state and from each other, then every religious group has a stake in the society. Each group needs the society to shelter its own distinctiveness.

But if each religion is to be protected, how can we know what is a religion. What is it that is to be protected? How can we identify the activities that are to be protected? Is any practice made in the name of religion to be permitted? What about the sacrifice of animals? Or even people? Two important questions need to be answered. First, what is the test of religion? (For instance, the American Selective Service laws say that a religious philosophy or a set of ethics is not sufficient to allow exemption from registration for military service.) Secondly, what behavior is outside the protection of constitutional guarantees of religious toleration because it is dangerous or outrageous in some respect, or not reasonably related to body of doctrine which can be classified as a religion? (An example of the former might be a doctrine calling for the ritualistic torture of animals; an example of the latter might be the insistence of a "deacon" that he was exempt from a local zoning ordinance prohibiting the erection of any TV or radio antenna higher than 35 feet from ground level in a residential area.)

The simulation which follows raises both of these questions. What is (or what should be) the test of religion? That is, what traits must a "religion" have to be protected by the Constitution of Atlantis? What behavior should be outside the protection of the Constitution? These questions cannot be answered by appeal to judges, precedent, etc. The Constitution itself is now open to amendment, as you will discover in the paragraphs which follow. You, as a member of the Constitutional Convention, must consider the wisdom of various proposals and alternatives, and *you must decide.*

The Setting

The Atlantis Constitution, like its American counterpart, contains a Bill of Rights section. While most of it is not relevant to our concerns, the section on religion is. That particular section is very similar to what is found in the U.S. Constitution. It reads:

Article VIII. Rights of the Citizens of Atlantis

Section 3. Neither the National nor Provincial Legislatures shall make any law respecting an establishment of religion, or prohibiting the free exercise thereof.

Several different religious groups that sprang up over the past dozen or so years have produced a public outcry over this clause. The nature of the problem is sketched below.

Reference was made in "Atlantis—The New Nation" to the Nature People and the problems they seem to present. The sect had its beginning in the United States in California, late in the 20th century, and spread quickly to other nations. Membership in Atlantis tends to be concentrated in Beta, as might be expected. As has been mentioned earlier, the religious practices of the Nature People stress nudity and openly displayed sexual behavior. For example, they have insisted that their children have a religious right not to wear clothes while attending school ("Clothing was invented by the devil—God brought Adam and Eve into the world naked and the return to the Garden of Eden will be possible only if people accept nudity"); they argue that school libraries should include books by authors of their persuasion so that children will not be corrupted by all that reading which espouses covering the body with clothing; their places of worship resemble theatres with live sex acts. Even the tolerant Betans began to feel that the situation was getting out of control when the national convention of the Nature People was held in Beta at the New Milano civic stadium. Originally the event was to be covered by several of the national television channels, but the sights and sounds were just too much even for these permissive times and reruns of old sitcoms were quickly substituted.

For conservative elements of Beta, this convention was the final straw. Restrictive legislation has been introduced in Beta's provincial legislature. The conservatives fear that Atlantis, and Beta in particular, soon will be drowning in a sea of sexual indulgence and moral turpitude. It is a total distortion of a protected right, conservatives insist, to argue that Nature People may, in the name of religious freedom, engage in sexual acts anywhere. Are the public parks to be available to them for their "religious rituals"? In order to protect one's children from being exposed to this behavior are we to assume that our only recourse is to stay away from all public parks? Are these groups free to engage in these "rituals" on public streets, in public buildings? Suppose a Nature People man and woman decide to "pray" in a restaurant, a department store, or even a Methodist Church? Are there to be no restrictions?

Another sect which has created problems for Atlantis has been the Church of the Spirit. The group believes that life's goals should be to search for tranquility and unity with all living things. It believes that current institutions are all corrupt: society, all governments, churches, professions, and especially the family. Therefore, its practitioners remove themselves from society, live together in communities where time is spent working for the community and seeking communion with the spirit. These communities are rigidly disciplined. Members arise each morning at 4:30 a.m., engage in morning exercises, eat a simple breakfast of brown rice and tea, have religious lessons for two hours, then work in the fields or perform chores. A simple lunch is followed by more work until sundown, another simple meal, and more lessons. The last event of each day consists of the smoking of hashish, to achieve total tranquility, then sleep. After two years of this rigorous life, members are encouraged to go out into the world and proselytize, especially among the young people. They receive no income and are expected to live on what they can get by begging. Any income they receive from the sale of flowers (picked from public gardens or from church gardens) and booklets about their religion is expected to be given back to the church.

The leader of this sect calls himself Reverend Dream, and not surprisingly the members have become known as the Dreamers. The sect has chapters worldwide and has attracted individuals of both sexes, of all races, and of diverse ethnic origins. Entire families have joined communities which are now located in every Atlantis province, although they are concentrated in Beta. All individuals are equal in the eyes of the group, and they are treated equally, which accounts for some of its appeal. Members are encouraged (critics say "forced") to give up all their earthly possessions to Reverend Dream, and as a result large amounts of wealth have been accumulated by the organization. These sums have been invested, first in real estate, then in industries which have supplied the communities of the Dreamers. The industries in turn have begun to sell their products to the general public, expanding constantly. The general public does not know whether to be most upset with the expanding industries, the ever expanding purchases of land, the capturing of the young, or the smoking of hashish.

Reaction to the Dreamers in the provinces of Atlantis has been varied. In some of the provinces there has been a tendency to ignore the Dreamers. This has not been true, however, in the areas where the Dreamer communities are located. There have been reports of beatings of Dreamers, of suspicious fires in Dreamer community houses, and of threats to Dreamer proselytizers. Where the cultural norms have stressed religious traditionalism, the citizenry has been very hostile, at all levels of society. When one of the agribusinesses was purchased by the Reverend Dream, the outrage reverberated right to the provincial legislature, and then to the Atlantis National Assembly. Similar anger has been expressed in Omega, for reasons which reflect the uniqueness of its culture (see "Atlantis—The New Nation"). Not surprisingly, the Omegan representatives reflect the anger of the people of Omega and share their values. They are demanding that "something should be done."

A third cult, smaller in size than either the Nature People or the Dreamers, exists only in the province of Delta. It is known as the Snake Cult. While for the most part its rituals and beliefs reflect accepted religious traditions, there is one part of its ceremony which has created problems for Delta officials. The Snake Cult members believe that if one truly believes in one's religion, then one can handle a cobra and the snake will not bite, or if one is bitten, then the believer will not be harmed by the venom. No one is ever forced to take part in this ritual, it is entirely voluntary. However, as part of the religious ceremony, individual members are encouraged "to come forth and test your faith," which involves handling a cobra. Inevitably, some people are bitten, some who are bitten die. Church leaders and members state publicly and privately that this ritual is none of the province's business. Young people under the age of 18 are not permitted to take part in snake handling, although they may be, and typically are, witnesses to the practice. The criticism comes from nonmembers and from some disenchanted former members who have lost loved ones. The question for Delta officials is whether or not snake handling comes under the protection of the "free exercise" clause.

Yet another religious group, known as the Defenders of the Faith, has appeared on the scene, thus far only in the Province of Gamma. There is widespread concern that, while the group is small in size at the moment, the appeal it offers, especially for youngsters between the ages of 12 to 19, will make it a problem everywhere.

The reason for its popularity goes back to a basic problem, perhaps even weakness, in industrialized societies. Some observers of industrialized cultures have suggested that there is a genuine problem in the way young people are reared, and its root is in the absence of a "rite of passage." Young people in many industrialized cultures are reared in a permissive way and may drift into adulthood without having encountered ways of "proving" that they are adults. There is no accepted practice or path which a young person can follow and know that the successful completion will result in a celebration of his or her adulthood. Thus the young must invent their own practices, many of which may be harmful to themselves or to society. Or, lacking knowledge of how to become an "adult," the young may drift into a perpetual state of juvenile behavior, escaping from a reality they do not or cannot understand by turning to drugs, alcohol, or aimless living. At least that is what some observers believe.

As an antidote for this problem, the Defenders of the Faith movement was started by a man and woman of great wealth, who have chosen to remain anonymous. They purchased a large area of land in a remote and rugged area of Gamma, and they endowed a trust to develop a program of training and education for the young. The emphasis of the education is a mixture of learning basic skills, Atlantis history, and fundamentalist religious beliefs. The training is of a paramilitary nature and emphasizes physical endurance. The culmination of the course is a two-week survival experience where one is required to live off the land with no assistance whatever. Some people fail the test, although they are permitted to take it as many times as they wish. Others, however, are not so fortunate, for they perish from the hardships of the experience or the natural dangers of the terrain and wildlife. The survivors are never allowed to forget that they have passed. They are indeed adults.

Supporters of the movement call attention to the benefits for society which accrue from more and more young people getting out into the open, surviving the rites of passage, acquiring basic skills, and becoming disciplined and responsible members of society with sound religious values. Critics argue that the paramilitary nature of the experience makes these young people ripe targets for some future leader who may offer continued opportunities for blind obedience. They have not been trained to think, the critics argue, only to obey. And the fact that most survive conveniently ignores those who are killed or are maimed for life by the experience.

Many commentators, editors, and publicists are denouncing the practices of these various groups, although some stress the good points of the Defenders of the Faith movement. The arguments put forth by the critics can be summarized as follows.

One does not have the right to do anything one wishes, anywhere one wishes to do it, justifying it in the name of religion. The "free exercise" clause is linked to religion, which, by customary definition, is "a system of beliefs and rituals centering on a supernatural being or beings." It is not enough merely to proclaim any act as religious—one might then be able to argue that rape was justifiable if committed as a religious act, or even human sacrifice, for that matter. There are tests which might be applied to determine whether or not actions fall within the protective cloak of the "free exercise" clause.

1. Since it is a religion which is being protected, there must be some connection between the actions claimed to be deserving of protection and a recognizable system of beliefs centering on the supernatural. A sect must therefore be able to provide evidence describing a system of beliefs. The burden is on the sect to demonstrate that it has a system of beliefs.

2. The sect must be able to show that the acts engaged in are intimately related to the beliefs, are in no way physically harmful either to the practitioners or to others, and are not dangerous to society's moral standards or laws. No one will argue that commerce in heroin is permissible just because it is done in the name of religion or because the profits go to a church. Similarly, if a religion insisted that its members inject heroin as a proof of faith, such practice would be forbidden.

3. No religious group has the right to inflict its practices on the public. Some rituals, while neither harmful to practitioners, nor offensive to community moral standards, are nevertheless irritating and even provocative when practiced publicly. An illustration would be the screaming denunciation of all other religions in Atlantis by Nature People. Roman Catholics, Greek Orthodox, Methodists, Moslems, and Jews, for exam-

ple, are all considered to be agents of the devil since these religions encourage people to be clothed. While the free exercise of religion and freedom of speech clauses would certainly protect the Nature People in the sanctity of their places of worship (except they don't really have any), there is no guarantee of protection if their denunciations occur in public places. Protecting society from riot in such situations is more important than the right of this religious group to denounce other religions in public.

Defenders of the religious groups offer a quite different and much more permissive definition of free exercise of religion as they counter the more traditional arguments. Free exercise of religion, they argue, means just what it says—freedom from interference by society. But, in addition, those who are more permissive disagree fundamentally with every traditionalist argument.

1. Contrary to the claims of the traditionalists, these religious groups do have a doctrine, a set of religious beliefs. For some, it is clearly religious rituals, symbols, or texts. For others, it may not be as highly organized, or complex, or written. But the practices are based on the beliefs—in the case of the Nature People, on a love of nature and a life lived as close to nature as possible. No animal, bird, or fish is required to give its life so that Nature People may live. No commercially processed foods are eaten. Foods are either eaten raw, or cooked only enough to make them edible. Home processing or preserving is permitted of vegetables and fruits. Nuts, cheese, and yogurt are important staple foods. Since fermentation is a natural process, home wine and beer making is encouraged. Distilled beverages are forbidden. As to the burden being placed on the sect to prove that there is a system of beliefs, how systematic was Christianity at its beginning? Can one argue that the parables of Jesus are a good example of the standard to be applied to judge whether a set of religious beliefs is entitled to the protection of the "free exercise" clause?

2. Critics of the religious groups argue that the acts engaged in must be intimately related to the beliefs, must in no way be physically harmful, nor can they be dangerous to the society's

moral standards or laws. As to the first test, the relationship between the behavior of these groups and their beliefs is obviously so close that no explanation or defense is required. Concerning the practices being harmful, the Nature People abhor violence of any kind, as do the Dreamers. The Defenders of the Faith harm no one. While some of those in the program may be harmed in the survival test, no one is compelled to do it. Anyone can opt out of the program at any time. In addition, it is the parents who must give their consent, and they are enthusiastic supporters, as are the graduates. Criticism tends to come from those who want Atlantans to be weak, and often this includes those who dropped out of the test.

Of course, the "free exercise" clause does not protect behavior which, under the guise of religious freedom, is harmful either to practitioners or the public. But nudity and public acts of sexual behavior are not harmful, in themselves, to anyone. The Nature People do not believe in either sadism or masochism, for these involve harm or injury. Another traditionalist comparison is that heroin commerce or use cannot be included in protected behavior under the guise of religious freedom. Again, this is a red herring argument. The Defenders of the Faith and the Snake Cult denounce drugs of all kinds. Perhaps the greatest threat they offer is not to societal moral standards but to the medical fraternity and the drug industry. The Nature People, for example, are even opposed to drugs as widely used as aspirin. They also oppose contraception and abortion. Just how, therefore, can they be a threat to anyone? Only the Snake Cult can be considered harmful to its members. The conflict is the classic one between society's concern to protect people from their own practices and the equally important concern that religious practices remain free of interference from government officials and private individuals. It is amazing, however, that society does not object when individuals kill or maim themselves or others in sports (racing, body contact sports, sky diving), but does object when a religious ritual is involved.

3. Finally, the critics state that no religious group has any right to inflict its practices on the public. But that is the whole point of civil rights—to protect minorities from majorities. Majorities

are powerful, minorities are weak. Do we wish to start the practice of having a referendum whenever the freedom of a minority is threatened? If the majority decreed that Thursday is the accepted day of worship, and required that no one work on that day, what would happen to Christians who worship on Sunday, or Seventh Day Adventists or Orthodox Jews who believe that Saturday is the correct day for worship? Must these individuals shut down their activities on Thursday just because the majority has so decreed? As for tolerance of, or even protection for, irritating and even provocative practices in public, that too is the essence of a civil liberty. In the words of the great American jurist Justice Oliver Wendell Holmes, freedom of speech means freedom for the thought we hate. It is the irritating, the unconventional, we must protect, for the conventional is always protected by the majority.

As if the "offensive" religious practices were not enough of a problem, there is one other dimension which adds complications. Atlantis grants tax exemptions to religious groups, as does the United States. Thus religious organizations are not subject to real estate taxes, to taxes on income which is devoted to the church and generated by the sale of religious books and pamphlets, and profits of businesses operated by religious organizations are not subject to corporate income taxes. Thus the anger felt by many Atlantis citizens is founded on both moral and economic grounds.

As can be seen, the religious practices of these four sects, and their economic implications, have been very disturbing to many citizens of Atlantis. As a result, varying events have been occurring throughout the nation. In the most conservative provinces (see "Atlantis—The New Nation"), especially those whose culture is heavily influenced by fundamentalist religions, congregations have been hearing angry, fire and brimstone sermons full of warnings of the wrath of God which will surely be felt if these immoral sects are not stamped out. Ministerial ire has been directed in particular at the Nature People and the Dreamers. Fundamentalist church members, worried parents, businesses, taxpayers, all feel threatened. In different ways and to different degrees, the practices of these sects seem to challenge the survival of a way of life. Across the nation, but especially in the more traditional provinces, demands are heard that the growing economic power and the siren-like appeal to the young of these groups be controlled.

Leaders of the business world, including agribusiness and banking, have horrifying visions of a Dreamer dominated society as the insidious tentacles of Reverend Dream's movement begin to capture banks, industries, and farmland. Labor leaders view the competition of what they see as "slave labor" in Reverend Dream's businesses as a direct threat to organized labor and the standard of living of working men and women. How can unionized companies compete, says one union leader, with companies owned by the Dreamers and staffed by religious "zombies" who work for nothing and live in communes? Parents, aroused by ministerial and media editorials, are upset by the threat which hangs over their families. The prurient temptations of the Nature People and the vegetative appeal of the Dreamers are matters of great concern. There is in the media and from the pulpits a constant drumbeat of frustration, of anger, of urgings that "something must be done."

Where the threats, both moral and economic, have seemed to be the most real, residents sometimes have taken action on their own. In some cases, local leadership has responded to citizen demands by authorizing police raids on Nature People "churches" or Dreamer communes, charging them with various violations of the law—possession of hallucinogenic substances, contributing to the delinquency of minors, lewd and lascivious public behavior, and so on. In most instances, the cases have been thrown out of court because of conflict with the Atlantis Constitution. More disturbing have been the illegal actions of local vigilante groups. While as yet there have been no deaths, there have been beatings of some leaders and members of both the Nature People and the Dreamers, and damage to their property as well.

Cooler heads have attempted to respond to this lawlessness with references to the long history of religious tolerance in Atlantis. The Atlantis Civil Liberties Union, for example, has been (as has its American counterpart) a dedicated defender of the helpless, the unpopular, the persecuted. It has attempted to provide, where necessary, defense lawyers in court cases involving the increasingly harassed sect members. Although in the public mind the Snake Cult and Defenders of the Faith seem to be less obnoxious, members find themselves caught up in the growing hostility to all religious sects which do not seem to fit into the norm of accepted religious practices. Curiously, at times the same person will defend one of the groups while angrily opposing another of the sects. Thus some of the defenders of the Nature People and the Dreamers (on the grounds of free exercise of religion) may at the same time be critical of the Snake Cult (because people may be harmed). Likewise, some of those who believe that the Defenders of the Faith Movement is good (because it claims to be based on fundamentalist religious traditions and patriotism) will oppose vigorously the other three sects as deviant destroyers of historic Atlantis values. So it goes. Consistency seldom has been one of the most prized of human traits, and Atlantis is no exception.

The Simulation

As in several other sections, the Amending Clause of the Atlantis Constitution is based on the American Constitution. The portion which is relevant at this time reads:

Article VIII Amending this Constitution

The Atlantis National Assembly, when two-thirds of both houses shall deem it necessary, shall propose amendments to this Constitution, or, on the application of the legislatures of two-thirds of the several provinces, *shall call a convention for proposing amendments,* which, in either case, shall be valid to all intents and purposes, as part of this Constitution, when ratified by the legislatures of three-fourths of the several provinces, or by conventions in three-fourths thereof . . .

As a result of the furor created by the activities of the four religious sects described earlier and the public clamor for action to deal with the problem, and following the procedure outlined above, a constitutional convention has been called. It should be understood that such a convention, having been called, is essentially a free agent. Under Atlantis law and traditions there are no restrictions on what the convention may propose in the way of revising the Constitution of Atlantis. (The same absence of limits applies should a constitutional convention be called in the United States. Perhaps for that reason alone, none has yet been called in American history.)

While there are no limits to what the convention can discuss or propose, the power to ratify proposed amendments rests either with the legislatures of the provinces or with special conventions chosen in each of the provinces for the purpose of deciding whether to ratify.

The Delegations

Since the Atlantis Constitution (like its American counterpart) does not specify the nature of the convention (i.e., method of representation, how delegates will be chosen, number of delegates), there was considerable debate on these topics in the Atlantis National Assembly. The less populated provinces objected strenuously to having representation based on population, the more heavily populated provinces understandably supported that concept. All other modes of representation were discussed and discarded until at last it became apparent that no consensus existed for any method of representation which seemed to give noticeable advantage to one or more of the provinces. After much bargaining, the following was agreed to:

1. The total number of delegates to be appointed will be determined at the time of the announcement of the creation of the Constitutional Convention. (Your instructor will convey this information to you.)

2. Each province will be entitled to *appoint* the same number of delegates.

3. No province may appoint substitute delegates in the event of the absence of a delegate.

4. On all votes on all subsidiary motions *prior to the final vote on the main motion, every delegate has the right to vote.* (e.g. amendments, procedural motions, etc.)

On the *final vote* on a main motion (i.e., the vote which approves or defeats that main motion), each provincial delegation has *only one vote*. Each delegation must determine how that vote will be cast.

5. A delegation vote may be split in half, but not into fractions smaller than half.

Stage One: Beginning the Simulation ——————

Your instructor will begin the simulation by identifying a location in the room for each delegation. The representatives of each delegation will then gather at these locations and seat themselves. It will be helpful if the representatives within each delegation introduce themselves to each other.

Your instructor may ask some members of the class to play advocacy roles for the several religious sects. The other members of the class may play themselves, but *they must not take positions which would be unrealistic for a representative of their province.* Other than that, everyone is free to use his or her own best judgment. When in doubt, ask yourself, "What is the plausible way for me to behave in that setting?" Follow a rule of reasonableness.

Your instructor will identify an individual to act as Speaker of the Constitutional Convention, and that person will be seated in front of the class. The Speaker will select someone from the class to serve as secretary. The secretary's task will be to record only *actions taken.*

The first order of business is for each delegation to choose someone to be spokesperson. No more than five minutes will be used for this.

Stage Two: Running the Simulation ——————

NOTE: A brief explanation of the principles of Parliamentary Procedure is located in the Appendix. You will find especially useful for reference during the simulation run the Rank Order of Commonly Used Motions (p. 219) and the Sequence of Motions chart (p. 219).

The Speaker will state:

"Several amendments to the Atlantis Constitution have been pro-posed in writing. I will place these motions on the floor *seriatim* (i.e., one at a time) for the consideration of the convention and ask if there is a second. If there is no second, this fact will be noted in the minutes, and I will then place the next motion on the floor." (NOTE: Your instructor may have decided to select only certain of the following motions for consideration. In that case, the Speaker will have been so advised.)

1. The Speaker will then state:

    "The first of the proposed amendments has been placed on the floor. It reads as follows:

    'To qualify for any exemption from taxation permitted by law, a religion must include:

    a. belief in a supreme being, and

    b. a written set of precepts for conduct.'
        The motion has not as yet received a second. The delega-tions will be allowed three minutes to caucus before I ask if there is a second." A maximum of three minutes will be al-lowed for the delegations to caucus.

Things to Keep in Mind: *Defining Religion (Atlantis Amendment 1)*

Is it enough that each "religion" decide for itself that it is indeed a religion? Or must criteria be specified? If so, what criteria? For example, must a religion have a body of written precepts? Must the followers of a religion exhibit some behavior in common (e.g., as a reflection of common precepts)? Must a religion have more than one adherent? If so, what is the minimum number that should be required?

Then the Speaker will ask, "Do I hear a second to the amendment?" If there is a second, discussion and possibly other motions will ensue.

When the Speaker believes that the convention is ready to vote, the Speaker will ask, "Do any of the delegations wish to caucus before the delegations cast their votes on the motion?" If requested, a three-minute caucus will be allowed.

The convention votes on the pending motion (each delegation casting one vote), and the Speaker announces the result.

2. The Speaker will then state:

"The second of the proposed amendments has been placed on the floor. It reads as follows:

'Nothing in this Constitution shall prevent either the national or provincial legislatures from curtailing actions which violate the accepted moral standards of the community.'

The motion has not as yet received a second. The delegations will be allowed three minutes to caucus before I ask if there is a second." A maximum of three minutes will be allowed for the delegations to caucus.

Things to Keep in Mind: *Language and Freedom (Atlantis Amendment 2)*

Why is the "Nothing shall prevent" format used in proposing amendments to the Constitution? The language of the Atlantis Constitution, like the First Amendment to the U.S. Constitution, is sweeping. It states that no law shall be passed restricting the freedoms of speech, press, religion, and peaceable assembly. Each of the issues in this simulation became a problem because this protective umbrella concept seems to go farther than some citizens think it should. In proposing a change of language, two methods are possible. One method is to tinker with the original language of the protective umbrella by substituting words, adding a phrase or two here or there, etc. For example, one might try to define the word *religion*. But this method runs substantial risks of uncertainty as the altered language then must be interpreted by courts. A more precisely controlled method of change is to leave intact the original language and then add a sentence which limits clearly the application of the original language in some respect. The net effect of this is to subtract from an important freedom the smallest amount of protection necessary to meet the societal demands for some subtraction.

Then the Speaker will ask, "Do I hear a second to the amendment?" If there is a second, discussion and possibly other motions will ensue.

When the Speaker believes that the convention is ready to vote, the Speaker will ask, "Do any of the delegations wish to caucus before the delegations cast their votes on the motion?" If requested, a three-minute caucus will be allowed.

The convention votes on the pending motion (each delegation casting one vote), and the Speaker announces the result.

3. The Speaker will then state:

"The third of the proposed amendments has been placed on the floor. It reads as follows:

'Nothing in this Constitution shall be interpreted to prevent the provincial legislatures from curtailing public nudity.'

The motion has not as yet received a second. The delegations will be allowed three minutes to caucus before I ask if there is a second." A maximum of three minutes will be allowed for the delegations to caucus.

Things to Keep in Mind: *Language and Freedom (Atlantis Amendment 3)*

As was explained in the "Things to Keep in Mind" for Amendment 2, if we wish to limit an important freedom, it is desirable to use language that subtracts the least amount of freedom required to achieve the purpose prompting the subtraction. That is why the language proposed above begins with "Nothing in this Constitution shall prevent.'' It is one way of subtracting the least amount from the umbrella of freedom provided by the statement of freedoms of the Atlantis Constitution.

Then the Speaker will ask, ''Do I hear a second to the amendment?'' If there is a second, discussion and possibly other motions will ensue.

When the Speaker believes that the convention is ready to vote, the Speaker will ask, ''Do any of the delegations wish to caucus before the delegations cast their votes on the motion?'' If requested, a three-minute caucus will be allowed.

The convention votes on the pending motion (each delegation casting one vote), and the Speaker announces the result.

4. The Speaker will then state:

''The fourth of the proposed amendments has been placed on the floor. It reads as follows:

'Nothing in this Constitution shall be interpreted to prevent the provincial legislatures from curtailing sexual behavior in locations and manners which may be observed by users of public lands or by lawful users of neighboring lands.'

The motion has not as yet received a second. The delegations will be allowed three minutes to caucus before I ask if there is a second.'' A maximum of three minutes will be allowed for the delegations to caucus.

Things to Keep in Mind: *Language and Freedom (Atlantis Amendment 4)*

As was explained in the ''Things to Keep in Mind'' for Amendment 2, if we wish to limit an important freedom, it is desirable to use language that subtracts the least amount of freedom required to achieve the purpose prompting the subtraction. That is why the language proposed above begins with ''Nothing in this Constitution shall prevent.'' It is one way of subtracting the least amount from the umbrella of freedom provided by the statement of freedoms of the Atlantis Constitution.

Then the Speaker will ask, "Do I hear a second to the amendment?" If there is a second, discussion and possibly other motions will ensue.

When the Speaker believes that the convention is ready to vote, the Speaker will ask, "Do any of the delegations wish to caucus before the delegations cast their votes on the motion?" If requested, a three-minute caucus will be allowed.

The convention votes on the pending motion (each delegation casting one vote), and the Speaker announces the result.

5. The Speaker will then state:

"The fifth of the proposed amendments has been placed on the floor. It reads as follows:

'Nothing in this Constitution authorizes the regulation or curtailment of activities which encourage respect for God, sound moral standards, self-discipline, and obedience to the laws of God and country.'

The motion has not as yet received a second. The delegations will be allowed three minutes to caucus before I ask if there is a second." A maximum of three minutes will be allowed for the delegations to caucus.

Things to Keep in Mind: *Language and Freedom (Atlantis Amendment 5)*

As was explained in the "Things to Keep in Mind" for Amendment 2, if we wish to limit an important freedom, it is desirable to use language that subtracts the least amount of freedom required to achieve the purpose prompting the subtraction. That is why the language proposed above begins with "Nothing in this Constitution shall prevent." It is one way of subtracting the least amount from the umbrella of freedom provided by the statement of freedoms of the Atlantis Constitution.

Then the Speaker will ask, "Do I hear a second to the amendment?" If there is a second, discussion and possibly other motions will ensue.

When the Speaker believes that the convention is ready to vote, the Speaker will ask, "Do any of the delegations wish to caucus before the delegations cast their votes on the motion?" If requested, a three-minute caucus will be allowed.

The convention votes on the pending motion (each delegation casting one vote), and the Speaker announces the result.

6. The Speaker will then state:

"The sixth of the proposed amendments has been placed on the floor. It reads as follows:
  'Nothing in this Constitution shall prevent the legislature of any province from enacting such legislation as is reasonably necessary to protect the health and safety of children under the age of 16.'
  The motion has not as yet received a second. The delegations will be allowed three minutes to caucus before I ask if there is a second." A maximum of three minutes will be allowed for the delegations to caucus.

Things to Keep in Mind: *Language and Freedom (Atlantis Amendment 6)*

As was explained in the "Things to Keep in Mind" for Amendment 2, if we wish to limit an important freedom, it is desirable to use language that subtracts the least amount of freedom required to achieve the purpose prompting the subtraction. That is why the language proposed above begins with "Nothing in this Constitution shall prevent." It is one way of subtracting the least amount from the umbrella of freedom provided by the statement of freedoms of the Atlantis Constitution.

Then the Speaker will ask, "Do I hear a second to the amendment?" If there is a second, discussion and possibly other motions will ensue.

When the Speaker believes the convention is ready to vote, the Speaker will ask, "Do any of the delegations wish to caucus before the delegations cast their votes on the motion?" If requested, a three-minute caucus will be allowed.

The convention votes on the pending motion (each delegation casting one vote), and the Speaker announces the result.

7. The Speaker then will state:

"The seventh of the proposed amendments has been placed on the floor. It reads:

'Property owned by a religious organization shall be exempt from taxation by Atlantis, its Provinces, or any of the political subdivisions.' "

Things to Keep in Mind: *Religion and Taxes*

What is especially at stake here is whether religious organizations will be required to pay local property taxes, but there is the additional issue of whether they should have to pay income taxes on the profits received from non-religious activities. As you can imagine, this is a very sensitive issue in Atlantis as it is in the United States. In Ohio, for example, only the property which is used for instructional, worship, or charitable purposes is exempt from local property taxes. Thus the schools, hospitals, and places of worship are not assessed local property taxes, but if any property is used for profit production, such as renting space to business, or charging rent for an apartment, then that property is taxed.

The tradition in Massachusetts, however, has been to exempt *all* property owned by a religious organization from taxation, whether it is used for instructional, worship, charitable, or income producing purposes.

In the United States there always has been a small minority opposed in principle to any tax exemptions for religious organizations. They are not opposed to such exemptions for charitable activities, but their opposition is quite firm to any tax exemption for property which is used for educational, instruction, or worship purposes.

Not surprisingly, Reverend Dream has been leading the fight to keep tax exemption for all the activities of the Dreamers. His claim is that all of the income produced by the many businesses owned by the Dreamers is used for religious activities. Reverend Dream's goal is to build a complete system of schools and universities all over the nation of Atlantis. In addition, there will be Dreamer hospitals, research institutes, and charities. In short, it is very difficult to dispute Reverend Dream's claim, except that his own lifestyle is hardly a testimonial to a life of self-denial.

Then the Speaker will ask, ''Do I hear a second to the amendment?'' If there is a second, discussion and possibly other motions will ensue.

When the Speaker believes that the convention is ready to vote, the Speaker will ask, ''Do any of the delegations wish to caucus before the delegations cast their votes on the motion?'' If requested, a three-minute caucus will be allowed.

The convention votes on the pending motion (each delegation casting one vote), and the Speaker announces the result.

Stage Three: Debriefing and Critique

Your instructor will inform you when this is to begin.

NOTE: Your instructor may ask you to complete and turn in the evaluation form which is located on the next page.

Evaluation Form **Simulation Seven**

1. In comparison with other courses, or portions of courses, which you have taken, how would you rate this simulation experience?

2. What do you consider to be the most important thing (or things) you learned from the simulation?

3. Was there anything about the simulation which you found disappointing?

4. Do you have any suggestions as to how the simulation might be improved?

5. Suppose a friend had a choice of introductory American Government sections, one of which used simulations such as the one you just experienced. The friend asks you whether he or she should choose the section offering the simulation. What would your advice be?

Please indicate whether your role was:
    _____ Very active (Speaker, outspoken person.)
    _____ Moderately active (Spoke once or twice, but was not very involved.)
    _____ Slightly active (Active only within the provincial discussions.)
    _____ Inactive (Observed the events, did not really participate in them.)

If more space is needed, the opposite side of this page may be used. If you wish to suggest changes or improvements in the simulation, please do so. Thank you.

Freedom for the Thought We Hate

A Dilemma for Locally Elected Decision Makers

*[Freedom of speech means] not free
thought for those who agree with us,
but freedom for the thought we hate.*

Justice Holmes
U.S. v. Schwimmer (1929)

The Introduction to Simulations Seven and Eight gave an overview of the place of freedom of speech in our lives. We saw there the dual importance of freedom of speech: (1) We saw its instrumental importance as an essential component of the democratic process, and (2) we also saw its importance as a personal freedom cherished by each of us for its intrinsic worth to our self expression and personal development. However, as was pointed out in that Introduction, assertions of the importance of freedom of speech, no matter how ringing and persuasive they may be, leave us uncertain of where we may find the outer limits of that freedom. Let us direct our attention, then, to that question—where are the outer limits of freedom of speech located?

The Limits of Freedom of Speech

The first step in exploring the limits of speech is to clarify the meaning of terms. Except as may be specifically mentioned below, the word *speech* will include both speaking and writing, and the phrase *freedom of expression* is interchangeable with the phrase *freedom of speech*.

The second step is to group the various problems into categories. One category consists of statements which are objectionable to some individuals because of their content, such as libel (discussed below), obscenity, writings or speeches which incite others to violence, or denunciation and ridicule of the religious faith of another person. A second category is objectionable to others because of the manner of delivery. Examples of the latter category include loud speakers mounted on trucks and blaring their message at 2:00 in the morning in a residential neighborhood, abusive graffiti painted on a wall or sidewalk, picketing of your home by a student complaining of a low grade you assigned to his term paper yesterday, or a personal confrontation made outrageously unacceptable by choice of location or timing. And, as is so often the case when analysis is applied to life, some problems seem to present a blend of the two categories.

Libel (a false and defamatory written statement) and slander (a false and defamatory spoken statement) have technical differences of considerable interest to lawyers who must advise a client, but they are equal in their relationship to the First Amendment to the United States Constitution. They are examples of restraints on freedom of speech in that the writer or speaker may be liable to pay damages for injury caused by a false and defamatory statement. These restraints are not affected by the First Amendment's "umbrella of protection." Since libel and slander can afford students a first rung on the ladder of understanding of the limits to freedom of speech, it is appropriate to begin the climb with a consideration of them.

Until the past several decades the general rule had been that neither libel nor slander was protected by the First Amendment. The reason for this is that libel or slander creates a dispute between two private parties, plaintiff and defendant, in a civil (as opposed to criminal) suit. The government is not a party to the dispute; it serves only to provide a forum (court of law) in which the dispute may be heard and decided. If the plaintiff wins, no imprisonment can result; an award of money as compensation for the injury to reputation is the only remedy likely to accrue to the plaintiff if the libel or slander is proven. Since the government is neutral in all this, the First Amendment, a restraint on government, has no applicability. This still is the general rule that determines the outcome of the great bulk of the cases, but in the past several decades an exception has been carved out with respect to one type of case. If the libelled or slandered party (plaintiff) is a public official, then a democracy's interest in the free flow of both information and opinion may override the personal interest of the official, even though he has become the victim of the false and injurious statement. In other words, the unfettered opportunity to criticize our officials is essential to the democratic process, and the First Amendment's protective umbrella has been extended by the Supreme Court to cover such criticism, whether true or false, provided only that the statement was not made with "actual malice," that is, "with knowledge that it was false or reckless disregard of whether it was false or not" (*New York Times Co. v. Sullivan, 376 U.S. 255,* 1964).

Notice that in the preceding paragraph the issue pertained to the content of the speech, not the manner of its presentation. Notice also, that the result of the principles described there is that persons can be held to account in a certain way for the content of their speech. Three other topic areas also seem to have some potential for challenging us with the problem of limiting speech because of its content. One rather narrow such area is the administration of justice. To illustrate with an example, suppose that a city newspaper editor, eager to see the conviction of an organized crime leader currently on trial in that city, published the names and addresses of jurors and urged readers to phone, write, or stop in person to tell the jurors' families how important a conviction would be. Would not that pose a serious threat to the fair administration of justice? A second area of possible limitation is obscenity. Is all writing and are all photographs, no matter what the content, no matter what the depths of vulgarity, depravity, and even cruelty portrayed therein, protected by the First Amendment? Or are there boundaries to the umbrella's protection? Finally, and most troublesome of all, we have the problem of speech which aims at sedition; speech which, to take but one example, is intended to encourage, and would have the effect of encouraging the overthrow of the government by violence. Here the agony of choice can be sharp indeed, for one man's sedition may be another man's patriotic reform. Moreover, all of the concern expressed earlier for the unfettered exchange of information and opinion in order to bolster democracy comes back to perplex us. If sedition, or political speech of any sort, is to be constrained by any boundary, the setting of that boundary must be a matter of the most profound gravity and exquisite precision. That is the burden of democracy.

When we turn to the second category of problems—problems of the manner of presentation of speech—will not the boundary setting task be distinctly easier? Cannot citizens take comfort in the knowledge that they are being true to their democratic principles by protecting the content of speech even though they insist on certain reasonable conditions for the manner of presentation? Alas, no such easy exit seems available. Consider, for example, the candidate for city council who wishes to spend Saturday promoting his candidacy by distributing campaign literature and shaking hands in a local shopping mall. If he is denied access to the mall for the purpose of distributing that campaign literature, can we truly say that speech is unfettered? Can it truly be said that the democratic processes are safe because the regulation is "merely" a regulation of the manner, not the content, of speech? To state the question is to answer it!

The Agony of Democratic Choice

Some of the dilemmas suggested above become even sharper when they appear amidst the complexity of real life settings. An extraordinarily poignant example of such a dilemma was taken from real life and became the basis for this simulation. The problem begins with recognition that freedom of political speech claims our highest loyalty, for the reasons adverted to earlier. The problem proceeds to a further recognition that a procession or parade is generally held to be a form of expression protected by the First Amendment. True, there may be reasonable constraints of a limited sort placed on parades in the interest of public safety. Regulation of time and route so as to minimize the disruption to traffic and maximize safety has been upheld by the U.S. Supreme Court at the same time the court was affirming the basic proposition that parades are a protected form of expression.

So far, so good, you may be saying at this point; the group seeking to spread its message accepts some modest constraints in the interest of public convenience and the safety of all, but it is free to convey whatever message it chooses. That is the democratic way! But now the problem proceeds to add another layer of difficulty, for the parading group will be the province's small but virulent Nazi Party, an organization taking its inspiration from the writings, the speeches, and the policies of the Nazi Party of Adolf Hitler. More particularly, the Nazis preach doctrines of intense patriotism coupled to an equally strong militarism, and they retain the Hitler notions of the destined supremacy of the "Aryan race." As a consequence of these beliefs they defend vigorously Hitler's policies of strength, conquest, and extermination of "inferior races." There is no proof that the Nazis of Atlantis have engaged in crimes of violence in their efforts to follow the doctrines of the Nazi Party, but they proclaim vigorously their belief in those doctrines as their inspiration and their hope for the future. Moreover, they deplore and ridicule "democratic decadence," and, though they refrain from expressing any timetable for change, they loudly and frequently express their hatred of inferior groups such as Omegans, blacks, Jews, and Polynesians.

Make no mistake about it! These doctrines, and the conduct with which they are intertwined in history, are about as offensive and appalling as anything can be. Moreover, the Nazis insist that their message must be conveyed by a parade through neighborhoods composed of heavy concentrations of various nonwhite groups plus a neighborhood that is overwhelmingly Jewish. Some insight into the severity of the problem posed by the Nazis' application for a parade permit can be gained from the realization that this is a group seeking to spread a political message inspired by a political regime which was responsible for the death camps at Auschwitz and Treblinka—a regime which produced the scene described by German engineer Herman Graebe in a sworn affadavit read at the Nuremburg War Crimes Trials. Outside the town of Dubno, on October 5, 1942, he witnessed the execution of part of the town's 5,000 Jews by the German military. The affidavit was read by Sir Hartley Shawcross, chief British prosecutor, in the course of the Nuremburg War Crimes Trials:

The people who had got off the trucks—men, women and children of all ages—had to undress upon the order of an S.S. man, who carried a riding or dog whip. They had to put down their clothes in fixed places, sorted according to shoes, top clothing, and underclothing. I saw a heap of shoes of about 800 to 1,000 pairs, great piles of under-linen and clothing.

Without screaming or weeping these people undressed, stood around in family groups, kissed each other, said farewells and waited for a sign from another S.S. man, who stood near the pit, also with a whip in his hand. During the fifteen minutes that I stood near the pit I heard no complaint or plea for mercy . . .

An old woman with snow-white hair was holding a one-year-old child in her arms and singing to it and tickling it. The child was cooing with delight. The parents were looking on with tears in their eyes. The father was holding the hand of a boy about 10 years old and speaking to him softly; the boy was fighting his tears. The father pointed to the sky, stroked his head and seemed to explain something to him. . . .

I walked around the mound and found myself confronted by a tremendous grave. People were closely wedged together and lying on top of each other so that only their heads were visible. Nearly all had blood running over their shoulders from their heads. Some of the people were still moving. Some were lifting their arms and turning their heads to show that they were still alive. The pit was already two-thirds full. I estimated that it contained about a thousand people. I looked for the man who did the shooting. He was an S.S. man, who sat at the edge of the narrow end of the pit, his feet dangling into the pit. He had a tommy gun on his knees and was smoking a cigarette.

The people, completely naked, went down some steps and clambered over the heads of the people lying there to the place to which the S.S. man directed them. They lay down in front of the dead or wounded people; some caressed those who were still alive and spoke to them in a low voice. Then I heard a series of shots. I looked into the pit and saw that the bodies were twitching or the heads lying already motionless on top of the bodies that lay beneath them. Blood was running from their necks.

The next batch was approaching already. They went down into the pit, lined themselves up against the previous victims and were shot.

Much of the Graebe affidavit can be found in William L. Shirer's *The Rise and Fall of the Third Reich*, New York: Fawcett World Library, 1962, pp.1252–53.

No matter what the Nazis of Atlantis may say, they deliberately choose to link their cause to one of the greatest catastrophes ever to befall mankind—the Holocaust and World War II. And the catastrophe was all the more horrible because it was not a cataclysmic act of nature, it was the intended consequence of the designs of men. This, then, is the dilemma for citizens torn between the claims of their commitment to democracy and the claims of their commitment to human decency. How should that dilemma be resolved? Must residents of the nonwhite neighborhoods accept the calculated offense of a parade proclaiming their unacceptability and unfitness for citizenship? Must the residents of a Jewish neighborhood endure the revival of those memories of agony and horror of the Holocaust? If not, will we not inflict a seriously damaging blow to the very democracy that shelters and celebrates the diversity of the community? What would you do?

The Setting

The facts of this simulation are based loosely on an actual incident which occurred in 1977 in Skokie, Illinois, a Chicago suburb having a high concentration of Jewish residents, including some survivors of Nazi death camps and numerous relatives of Jews who died in the death camps. A splinter group of the American Nazi Party applied for a parade permit in Skokie, and the events and legal battles which followed attracted national attention. ("The Skokie Case," as it has come to be called, is recounted in fascinating detail by David Hamlin in the *Nazi/Skokie Conflict: A Civil Liberties Battle*, Beacon Press, 1980.)

The first of the four ingredients in our simulation is the Atlantis Civil Liberties Union (the ACLU) which, like its American counterpart, has a long and honored history of defending diverse views, especially views of unpopular individuals and minorities. The American Civil Liberties Union, for example, has defended Jehovah's Witnesses, atheists, the Ku Klux Klan, Communists, Nazis, and individuals accused of crimes when a basic civil right was involved. At times it has provided defense attorneys; at other times it has offered amicus curiae (friend of the court) briefs, which provide a background explanation of important legal or constitutional principles involved in a particular case. The ACLU is not an integral part of the legal system, nor is it subservient to or directed or influenced by any political party, interest group, or ideology. Because it will or has defended Communists, it has been accused of being either Communist dominated or Communist sympathizers. But when it defended Nazis, a similar accusation was heard. Thus, it was labelled atheistic when defending atheists, pro Ku Klux Klan when defending the KKK, and so on. It is remarkable that this extremely difficult, often thankless, yet significant role has been assumed by an organization entirely dependent for funds on the willingness of many individual donors. In the drama about to unfold before you the ACLU is again to play its controversial role as defender of an unpopular group.

A second ingredient is the Jewish community. While other groups can argue that they too have experienced discrimination and persecution (this is certainly true of the Seventh Day Adventists in both Nazi Germany and the Soviet Union, or the gypsies in Nazi Germany), perhaps no people have suffered so continuously over such a long period of history as the Jews. One can find horror stories concerning their experiences in almost every country and in every period of history. Just as a single example, in Europe in the Middle Ages, the occasion of a missing child would at times evoke rumors of Jews eating gentile children, and this would be followed by persecution, often torture and death. Given such a history, it is not surprising that Jews are very sensitive to issues of fairness and justice and to the preservation of the rights of individuals. For these reasons, Jews have been important to the ACLU by their contributions of money, energy and, in many instances, legal talent.

The third ingredient of this simulation, modelled as it is on the Skokie case, is the Atlantis National Socialist Party (the Nazis). Beneath the benign public posture which the Nazis present is a virulent hatred of Jews, blacks, Omegans, and any other ethnic group which is not Caucasian. While the repeated half-truths, distortions, and lies about these groups (such as "all Jews are rich," or "the Omegans and blacks are going to destroy the purity of the Caucasian race") seem bizarre to the outside observer, to the Nazis the statements may provide a comforting explanation for personal failures or economic troubles.

As a final ingredient we have the areas of the city inhabited by Jewish and Omegan residents. Here we find families, clusters of families, and neighborhoods populated by descendants of people who have experienced the horrors of the Holocaust and Hitler's Storm Troopers; and Omegans, who have suffered from discrimination in employment and housing and who have been targets of abuse and hatred from prejudiced segments of the population. The TV documentaries, the anniversaries of the release of the survivors of Dachau, Treblinka, and Auschwitz, remind the current victims of Nazi propaganda of what the future could bring. Here is a population whose greatest fear is that it might happen again.

The Issue

The Nazi Party has an active membership of about 25 individuals, with perhaps another 25 individuals who seem to share some of the beliefs of the party. Their main objective seems to be to call attention to themselves, and they always endeavor to get media coverage for all their events. Their small number, however, does not persuade the city's Jewish, Omegan, or black communities of the insignificance of the party, especially when the members seem to delight in holding fairly frequent parades through predominantly

Jewish, black, or Omegan neighborhoods. And this is exactly what the party leader of the Nazi Party has now proposed to the City Manager: a parade permit for an evening (8–10 p.m.) torch light march through the city. The parade route will take them on side streets through several Jewish, black, and Omegan neighborhoods. Because these are not heavily traveled streets, the Nazis know that the permit cannot be denied for reasons of traffic congestion.

City ordinances have given the authority to issue parade permits to the City Council, which must approve them by resolution. Council in the past has based parade permit decisions on traffic congestion considerations. Council—along with the manager—has responsibility for maintaining public safety also.

The leadership of the Jewish, black and Omegan communities are outraged. Echoes of the Holocaust and Hitler fill the air. Jewish leaders have stated quite bluntly that "never again will the Nazis be permitted to march in Jewish neighborhoods, screaming anti-Semitic slogans." They promise to resist with all force necessary. The black community leaders echo these sentiments, as do the Omegans.

The Atlantis Civil Liberties Union has promised to support the Nazi Party request for a parade permit since the rights of speech and assembly, guaranteed by the Atlantis Constitution, are involved. The Jewish, black, and Omegan leaders, as might be imagined, have not viewed the ACLU role in this matter with either sympathy or affection.

Following standard procedures, the Nazi Party leader has submitted the parade permit request to the City Manager, who in turn has instructed the Clerk to place the item on the Council agenda for a special meeting called for the purpose of considering this issue. The City Manager must make a recommendation as to whether the request, if granted, will create a traffic hazard, and what special instructions should be appended to any approval so as to assure public safety.

The Simulation Roles

1. Member, City Council
2. Member, City Council

3. Member, City Council

4. Member, City Council

5. Member, City Council

6. Member, City Council

7. Mayor (presides at council meetings; also has a vote on each issue before council)

8. City Manager. Available to advise the Mayor and other Council Members regarding administrative details such as traffic rerouting, police measures to be taken to avoid violence, etc.

9. Resident in area through which Nazis plan to march. Descendant of one of the survivors of Hitler's death camps. Lost grandparents and all aunts and uncles.

10. Resident in area through which Nazis plan to march. Now elderly, but was a child at the time of World War II. Escaped the death camps only because parents were able to get a Danish man and woman to provide shelter (and hiding space from the Gestapo). Parents were put to death.

11. Resident in area through which Nazis plan to march. Atlantis native born. Is late middle-aged. All relatives who were in Germany at the time of Hitler died in the death camps.

12. Resident in area through which Nazis plan to march. His or her grandparent, now very old and living alone, is the only family member to survive the pogrom in Warsaw, Poland.

13. Atlantis born. Parents were German born and had left the country in 1920, but had returned to Germany in 1935 for a visit to the homeland. Both were arrested by the Gestapo, separated, and sent to work at different labor camps. Father died while working in the mines. Mother was sent to a death camp in 1945 and saved when the American army overran that area. Mother moved to the U.S. and then later emigrated to

Atlantis and lived with her child and grandchildren until her death.

14. ACLU attorney. Successful lawyer who has strong convictions about the need to defend minority groups, even though they are unpopular. Viewed by colleagues as brilliant, a lawyer's lawyer.

15. ACLU attorney. Has a long established, successful law practice with numerous wealthy clients. Head of local Anti-Defamation League.

16. Retired Head of the N.A.A.C.P.

17. Current Head, N.A.A.C.P.

18–22. Members, N.A.A.C.P.

23. Party leader, Atlantis National Socialist Party.

24. Asst. leader, Atlantis National Socialist Party.

25. Asst. leader, Atlantis National Socialist Party.

26. Retired Head of Anti-Defamation League of B'nai B'rith.

27. Rabbi

28. Catholic Priest

29. Minister, Presbyterian Church

30. Resident in area through which Nazis plan to march. Born in Omega and moved to this city some 10 years ago to find employment. Has experienced discrimination many times in search for housing and employment.

31. Resident in area through which Nazis plan to march. Born in Omega and moved to this city very recently to find employment. Was recently severely beaten by a gang of young

toughs who were thought by some to be Nazis, but no firm identification ever was made.

32–37. Black residents of area through which Nazis plan to march.

38–43. Black residents living outside the march area.

44–49. Jewish residents living outside the march area.

50–55. Catholic residents living outside the march area.

56–61. Omegan residents living outside the march area.

62–67. White Protestant residents living outside the march area.

68–70. Muslim residents living outside the march area.

71–72. Hare Krishna residents living outside the march area.

73–75. Residents with no religious preference living outside the march area.

NOTE: Members of the class will be seated according to ethnic identity and residential area. Specific instructions will be provided before the simulation begins.

The Simulation

Stage One: Running the Simulation————————

NOTE: A brief explanation of the principles of Parliamentary Procedure is located in the Appendix. You will find especially useful for reference during the simulation run the Rank Order of Commonly Used Motions (p. 219) and the Sequence of Motions chart (p. 219).

The Mayor will state:

"The Alpha City Council will come to order. The only business to be conducted at this special meeting of Council is to consider the request of the Atlantis Nazi Party for a parade permit to hold a torch light march. The City Manager has indicated that the route of the march will be on side streets, and since the march is to be held at night, there is no danger of traffic congestion.

"The following procedure will be used. Members of Council will be given an opportunity to ask questions of the applicants (or their attorneys) and of the city staff. The purpose of this segment is to inform council. Members of Council should refrain at this time from discussing the issue among themselves. A period of not more than 10 minutes will be allowed for these questions.

"Opportunity will then be offered to the public to comment. Persons wishing to speak must obtain recognition from the presiding officer before speaking, and all remarks must be addressed to the Council and to the presiding officer.

"Following the public input, Council will again have an opportunity to review and discuss the issue and ask additional questions."

Council must then decide the question of granting the parade permit no later than three minutes prior to the end of the class period.

The Mayor will then state, "The floor is now open for discussion by Members of Council."

After 10 minutes, the Mayor will then state, "Ten minutes have now elapsed. I will now open the discussion to those in the audience."

The Mayor will then state, "The time for public input has now elapsed." (Your instructor will indicate the amount of time to be allowed for public input, probably in the range of 15–20 minutes.) "Council will now consider the question of granting a parade permit. Do I hear a motion?"

Following that, the discussion by Council members (including possible amendments) will continue.

No later than three minutes prior to the end of the class period, the Mayor will interrupt the discussion (if it has continued to this point) and announce that debate must end and a vote taken immediately. A simple majority of those present and voting is required to pass any motion.

Things to Keep in Mind: *Role Playing*

1. Members of Council and the City Manager may play themselves.

2. The other participants in the simulation must ask themselves what stand is required by the role they have been asked to play.

Stage Two: Debriefing and Critique

Your instructor will inform you when this is to begin.

NOTE: Your instructor may ask you to complete and turn in the evaluation form located on the following page.

Evaluation Form Simulation Eight

1. In comparison with other courses, or portions of courses, which you have taken, how would you rate this simulation experience?

2. What do you consider to be the most important thing (or things) you learned from the simulation?

3. Was there anything about the simulation which you found disappointing?

4. Do you have any suggestions as to how the simulation might be improved?

5. Suppose a friend had a choice of introductory American Government sections, one of which used simulations such as the one you just experienced. The friend asks you whether he or she should choose the section offering the simulation. What would your advice be?

6. Please indicate whether your role was:
   _____ Member of council, mayor, city manager, ACLU attorneys.
   _____ Outspoken person who lived in the march area.
   _____ Outspoken person who lived in the non-march area.
   _____ Less active person who lived in the march area.
   _____ Less active person who lived in the non-march area.

If more space is needed, the opposite side of this page may be used.

A Brief Introduction to Parliamentary Rules

Probably each of us has heard, at some time or other, an individual say, "Who needs parliamentary rules? They only complicate the decision-making process." Unfortunately, that opinion is the exact opposite of the truth. The purpose and the effect of parliamentary rules is to simplify the process of decision making in situations where the possibility of disagreement makes us sensitive to the need for orderly (and thereby less abrasive) decision procedures. Only when the decision-making group is small and unusually like-minded can the need for rules of order be avoided. In other situations, without rules of order, either there will be chaos, or one or two very assertive individuals will attempt to pressure the group to approve goals preferred by the assertive ones. Putting the matter another way, in the absence of rules, we probably will face a choice between nondemocratic decision making on the one hand or confusion on the other. Indeed, you may have found yourself in just such a situation at some time in the past.

Having said that, however, it does not follow that each of us needs to know every word of *Robert's Rules of Order*. For most of us it is sufficient that we understand merely the basics, and that is what is presented here. In the several pages which follow we have presented simplified and basic rules to assist your ability to function effectively in the *Atlantis* simulations.

Parlimentary Rules for the Beginner

In order to understand well the operation of parliamentary rules of order, we need to look at their purposes. It is clear at the outset that one of the most basic purposes is orderly decision making. While that purpose may be self-explanatory, along with it goes the additional purpose (usually unspoken) of maintaining the group as a continuing organization. If the decision-making processes are too disruptive, this latter purpose may be frustrated.

We also need to understand two terms which often are confused but which should be distinguished: majority and consensus. The term "majority" refers to more than fifty percent of a group. If, in voting on some issue, some persons abstain, the majority (unless the organization's rules state otherwise) is computed on the basis of the total number of persons voting, not on the basis of the total membership. Thus, in a group of 100 persons, if only 50 voted, a majority would mean 26 persons.

The term "consensus" is more slippery, for it has two meanings. The older (and we think more useful) meaning is "of agreement" or "harmony." More recently, some persons have tried to use "consensus" as though it is a synonym for "majority," but this use loses the flavor of "broad agreement" or "harmony" that distinguishes a consensus decision from a mere majority decision. We prefer to maintain the distinction between the two terms so that we can use the term "majority" in more or less of a legal sense while reserving "consensus" to direct our attention toward the undoubted social science truth that organizations that must make a series of decisions by very close votes probably are in danger of disintegration. To carry our point one more step, although the goal of organizations is to achieve consensus so that the cohesiveness of the organization is reinforced, the legal mechanism for doing so usually must be the principle of "majority rule." (Perhaps at this point you have realized that some organizations distinguish between ordinary majority and extra-large majority on a few issues. Indeed, this point is crucial to an understanding of the process of constitutional amendment in the United States and in most of the states of the United States. Thus when it comes to bringing about change in our most fundamental law, the Constitution, we require majorities greater than merely "more than half.")

The most fundamental principles which underlie all parliamentary rules are these:

1. The goal of every organization is to attempt to achieve agreement by as large a margin as possible (i.e., by a near consensus)

on each issue. The agreement (or near consensus) may be to revise, to postpone, to approve, or to disapprove the issue.

2. Minorities have a right to be heard, but they do *not* have the right to rule.

3. Majorities have an obligation to let minorities be heard, but ultimately it is the majority that must rule.

4. Only one main motion (that is, one issue) can be placed on the floor (that is, can be considered by the organization) at one time.

The purpose of the rules of order is to put into practice these fundamental principles. Thus if you keep the principles in mind, you will find that the rules of order are really very logical and based on common sense. A half-dozen illustrations follow:

1. In order to gain a majority, the main motion as originally proposed may need to be amended.

2. Each amendment that is put on the floor thus gives the organization a choice: does it prefer the original main motion or does it prefer the main motion as it would read if it were amended?

3. There are times when even the proposed amendment may seem to require a revision (that is, an amendment to the amendment) in order to satisfy a majority of those voting.

4. When a main motion and one or more additional motions (such as amendments) are on the floor (that is, none of them has been passed or defeated yet), the last motion proposed is the first motion to be considered. Remember: the last shall be first.

5. Parliamentary rules presume that some motions have greater immediacy than others, and so there is a rank order to motions. In addition to the main motion and possible amendments, motions can suggest various procedural steps, such as closing debate, or postponing consideration, or adjourning the meeting. You will find on page 219 a table which shows the rank order of a few of these procedural motions. (While many more proce-

dural motions can be found in a parliamentary reference book, these listed motions are the ones you are most likely to need. If more information is needed, your instructor will assist you.) If you look at the order of motions on page 219, you will note that the lowest ranking motion is the main motion, the highest is the motion to adjourn. As the table shows, all other motions fall somewhere between these. The chart on page 219 explains how this works.

6. There is another group of motions, called incidental motions. They are listed separately on page 219. Again, you will find listed there only the most commonly used incidental motions. As the name implies, the motions are incidental to the main motion and thus are outside the rank order of motions. Incidental motions may be offered at any time.

There you have the basics. Now, here are some words to use.

Putting a Motion on the Floor

MEMBER A: "Mr. (or Madame) Speaker."
SPEAKER: "Member A."
MEMBER A: "I move that our class pass a resolution urging our instructor to postpone the next exam until December 10."
SPEAKER: "You have heard the motion; is there a second?"
MEMBER B: "I second the motion."
SPEAKER: "It has been moved and seconded that our class pass a resolution urging our instructor to postpone the next exam until December 10. Is there any discussion?"
MEMBER C: "Mr. (or Madame) Speaker."
SPEAKER: "Member C."
MEMBER C: "December 10 is a very poor choice of a date. I move to amend the motion by substituting December 17 for December 10."
SPEAKER: "You have heard the amendment; is there a second?"

(No one seconds the amendment.)

> SPEAKER: "The proposed amendment dies for a lack of a second. Is there further discussion on the original motion?"

(Discussion follows, and perhaps other amendments will be proposed.)

Getting to the Vote on a Motion

The simplest way to do this is for the Speaker to sense that discussion has ended and say:

> "Are you ready to vote? If so, the motion is (states the motion). All in favor say 'aye.' Opposed 'no.' " (The Speaker announces the result of the vote.)

Another way is for a member, after receiving recognition from the Speaker, to say:

> "I move we vote immediately." (Or, "I move the previous question.")

This motion requires a second and a two-thirds affirmative vote of those voting on the issue. If the motion to "vote immediately" is approved by the required two-thirds affirmative vote, the Speaker announces this fact and immediately states:

> "The motion to vote immediately on the pending issue has been approved. We will therefore vote at once on whether our class approves the sending of a resolution to our instructor urging that the next exam be postponed until December 10. All in favor say 'aye.' All opposed say 'no.' The motion passes."

NOTE: There is a common misconception that calling out "Question!" will require the speaker to end the discussion. It does not. In the face of the desire of some members to continue debate, a two-thirds majority is required to end discussion. The speaker may, however, take the opportunity to say: "The question has been called. Are you ready to vote?" This calls attention to the fact that someone is getting impatient, but it does not stop debate unless there is general belief that the time to vote has arrived.

Other motions may be needed, and you will find the information you need on page 219. However, our experience suggests that the preceding dialogue will cover most of the situations you will encounter.

Parliamentary Rules: *Concluding Points*

1. When a main motion has been offered and seconded, no other main motion can be offered until the first main motion has been passed, postponed, referred to committee, or defeated.

   Summary point: Only one main motion can be discussed at one time.

2. When an amendment to the main motion has been offered and seconded, a second amendment *to the main motion* cannot be offered until the first amendment has been passed or defeated. (An amendment by itself cannot be postponed or referred to committee. The main motion must be included in such actions.)

   Summary point: Only one amendment to the main motion can be discussed at one time.

3. When an amendment to the amendment has been offered and seconded, a second amendment *to the amendment* cannot be offered until the first amendment has been passed or defeated.

   Summary point: Only one amendment to the amendment can be discussed at one time. The amendment to the amendment must relate directly to the amendment.

4. One may *not* amend the amendment to the amendment.

   A diagram of the preceding follows in the Sequence of Motions chart.

Rank Order of Commonly Used Motions

Motions	Needs Second?	Debatable?	Vote Required
"I move we adjourn the meeting."	Yes	No	Majority
"I move we take a recess for . . . minutes."	Yes	No	Majority
"I move we table the motion on the floor" (i.e., to postpone consideration temporarily).	Yes	No	Majority
"I move the previous question" (i.e., to vote immediately).	Yes	No	Two-thirds
"I move we limit debate on this motion."	Yes	No	Two-thirds
"I move to amend the motion by . . ."	Yes	Yes	Majority
"I move . . ." (the main motion).	Yes	Yes	Majority

NOTE: The above motions are in rank order, highest at the top of the list. Thus:

1. If a main motion is on the floor, no other main motions can be offered until the first one has been passed, defeated, or tabled.
2. A motion of higher rank takes precedence over motions of lower rank. This means, for example, that a motion to vote immediately must be passed or defeated before the motion to limit debate can be placed on the floor.
   Another example would be that if the motion to adjourn has been placed on the floor, it must be defeated before an amendment to a motion can be introduced.

Incidental motions which can be introduced at any time:

- Point of order (requires no second, nor any vote).

- Parliamentary inquiry (requires no second, nor any vote).

- Withdraw a motion (requires no second, nor any vote. If someone objects to the motion being withdrawn, the Speaker will immediately ask for a vote on the matter of the withdrawal of the motion, and a majority will decide).

Sequence of Motions

Main motion: "I move that each province of Atlantis have two representatives in the Upper House of the National Assembly."

  └─Amendment to the main motion: "I move to amend by adding the phrase 'elected at-large.' "

    └─Amendment to the amendment: "I move to amend the amendment by substituting the words 'by district' for 'at-large!' "

      └─Amendment to the amendment to the amendment: NOT PERMITTED